Advanced Placement
U. S. History 1
The Evolving American Nation-State
1607–1914

Roberta J. Leach

Augustine Caliguire

Student Edition

Roberta J. Leach, social studies teacher, who earned her doctorate in history at Carnegie Mellon University, has conducted A.P. U.S. history workshops. She is coauthor of eleven Center for Learning curriculum guides in social studies.

Augustine Caliguire, who earned his M.A. at John Carroll University, has taught world and American history at both the secondary and university level.

The Publishing Team

Rose Schaffer, M.A., President/Chief Executive Officer
Bernadette Vetter, M.A., Vice President
Lora Murphy, M.A., Vice President, Social Studies Division
Amy Richards, M.A., Editor

Cover Design

Krina K. Walsh, B.S.I.D.

List of credits found on Acknowledgement page beginning on 254.

Copyright © 1997 The Center for Learning.
Reprinted 2003.
Manufactured in the United States of America.

The worksheets in this book may be reproduced for academic purposes only and not for resale. Academic purposes refer to limited use within classroom and teaching settings only.

ISBN 1-56077-500-9

Contents

                                               Page   Handout

Part 1: Colonial America

1. The Three Colonial Sections—One Society or Three? 5 1
2. From Authority to Individualism 11 2
3. Colonial Exploitation—A Matter of Perception 16 3
4. Democracy in Colonial Wethersfield, Connecticut 23 4
5. British Colonial Policy—A Tradition of Neglect 33 5
6. The Colonies by 1763—A New Society? 39 6

Part 2: Establishing the Nation

7. The Path to Revolution, 1763-1776 .... 46 7
8. The Declaration of Independence 54 8
9. The Effects of the American Revolution 57 9
10. The Articles of Confederation—The Challenge of Sovereignty 65 10
11. The Constitution—Balancing Competing Interests 69 11
12. Foundations of American Foreign Policy 75 12
13. The Development of Political Parties 79 13
14. The Role of the Judiciary in the Creation of the National State ... 86 14
15. Coming Together—Nationalism Ascendant 91 15

Part 3: Solidifying the American Nation-State

16. The End of Homespun—The Early Industrial Revolution 96 16
17. The Early Industrial Revolution—
    Maintaining a Sense of Community 102 17
18. The Evolution of Democracy from Jefferson to Jackson 109 18
19. Purifying the Nation 118 19
20. The Mexican War—Was It in the National Interest? 122 20
21. Enlarging the National State 130 21
22. Compromise and Conflict—The Road to War 140 22
23. Abolition—The Role of the Individual in Effecting Change 145 23
24. The "Failure" of Radical Reconstruction 151 24

Part 4: Developing the American Nation-State

25. The Emergence of Industrial America 157 25
26. The Growing Economic Crisis of the Late Nineteenth Century 161 26
27. National Government in the Late Nineteenth Century—
    A Sham of Democracy 171 27
28. The Philosophy of the Industrialists 177 28
29. The Impact of Industrialization on Workers and Their Families.... 184 29
30. Labor Unions—The Failure to Gain Public Acceptance 187 30
31. The Farmers' Dilemma—To Produce or Not to Produce 195 31
32. The Populist Movement—The Value of Third Parties 203 32
33. Divergent Paths to Equality for African Americans 209 33
34. Arts in the Gilded Age 215 34
    Arts in the Gilded Age—An Interpretation 216 35

Part 5: Transition to Modernity—Imperialism and Progressivism

35. International Perspectives 221 36
36. Researching the Causes 227 37
37. A Foreign Policy for a New Age 234 38
38. Leaders of the Progressive Movement 239 39
39. *The Jungle* and the Progressives 244 40
40. Progressivism—Liberal Reform or Conservative Reaction?............. 252 41

Part 1
Colonial America

Part 1 analyzes the political, economic, social, and philosophical foundations of colonial America. You will compare and contrast the three sections of colonial America and also assess the extent to which the colonies developed a society different from that of the mother country by the end of the French and Indian War. In this unit, you will learn about this country's British heritage as well as how the colonies modified British institutions to the point that reconciliation seemed impossible after the French and Indian War.

At the conclusion of the unit, you should be able to answer the following basic questions:

- To what extent did the three sections of colonial America share common institutions and philosophies?

- What philosophical forces developing in colonial America weakened authoritarianism and created a climate for individual freedom?

- Although colonial Americans criticized the British for exploitation, how did they rationalize their own exploitation of blacks, women, and Native Americans?

- To what extent did democracy develop in colonial America?

- Why couldn't the British successfully reverse a tradition of neglect after the French and Indian War?

- In what respects did the colonies develop political, economic, social, and religious views inconsistent with their colonial status?

Advanced Placement U.S. History 1
Lesson 1
Handout 1 (page 1)

Name_____
Date_____

The Three Colonial Sections—One Society or Three?

Part A.

Study the accompanying maps to answer the following questions. In each instance, write the letter of the correct response, identify the map (or maps) containing the information, and cite specific evidence that supports the answer.

_____ 1. The nationality that was most common in all the colonies was
   a. German
   b. Scotch-Irish
   c. English
   d. Africans

_____ 2. The colonial section with the least variety of economic activity was
   a. South
   b. Middle Colonies
   c. New England

_____ 3. The colonial section with the most diversity of religions was
   a. New England
   b. Middle Colonies
   c. South

_____ 4. Judging from the maps on Religious Denominations and National Origins, which section had the widest range of languages and cultures?
   a. New England
   b. Middle Colonies
   c. South
   d. Frontier

_____ 5. Which of the following factors best tied the colonists together?
   a. Religion
   b. Trade
   c. Language

_____ 6. Which of the following best reflected the presence of England in all sections of the colonies?
   a. Anglican Church
   b. Slavery
   c. Fishing

_____ 7. Which colonial section best reflected the melting pot of nationalities?
   a. South
   b. New England
   c. Middle Colonies

_____ 8. Which section of the colonies had the least urban development?
   a. South
   b. Middle Colonies
   c. New England

© COPYRIGHT, The Center for Learning. Used with permission. Not for resale.

Advanced Placement U.S. History 1
Lesson 1
Handout 1 (page 2)

Name_____
Date_____

Part B.

To conclude this activity, answer the following:

1. List at least four similarities among the three sections of colonial America.

2. List at least four differences among the three sections of colonial America.

3. A society is characterized by similar values, mutual interests, shared institutions, and a common culture. Consider the following question: To what extent would it be accurate to say that the New England, Middle, and Southern Colonies had merged to create a single American society by the outbreak of the Revolution? Assume that your teacher has asked you to write a four-page paper on this question. Brainstorm questions for which you need answers in order to formulate a carefully considered response to this question.

© COPYRIGHT, The Center for Learning. Used with permission. Not for resale.

Advanced Placement U.S. History 1
Lesson 1
Handout 1 (page 3)

Name_____
Date_____

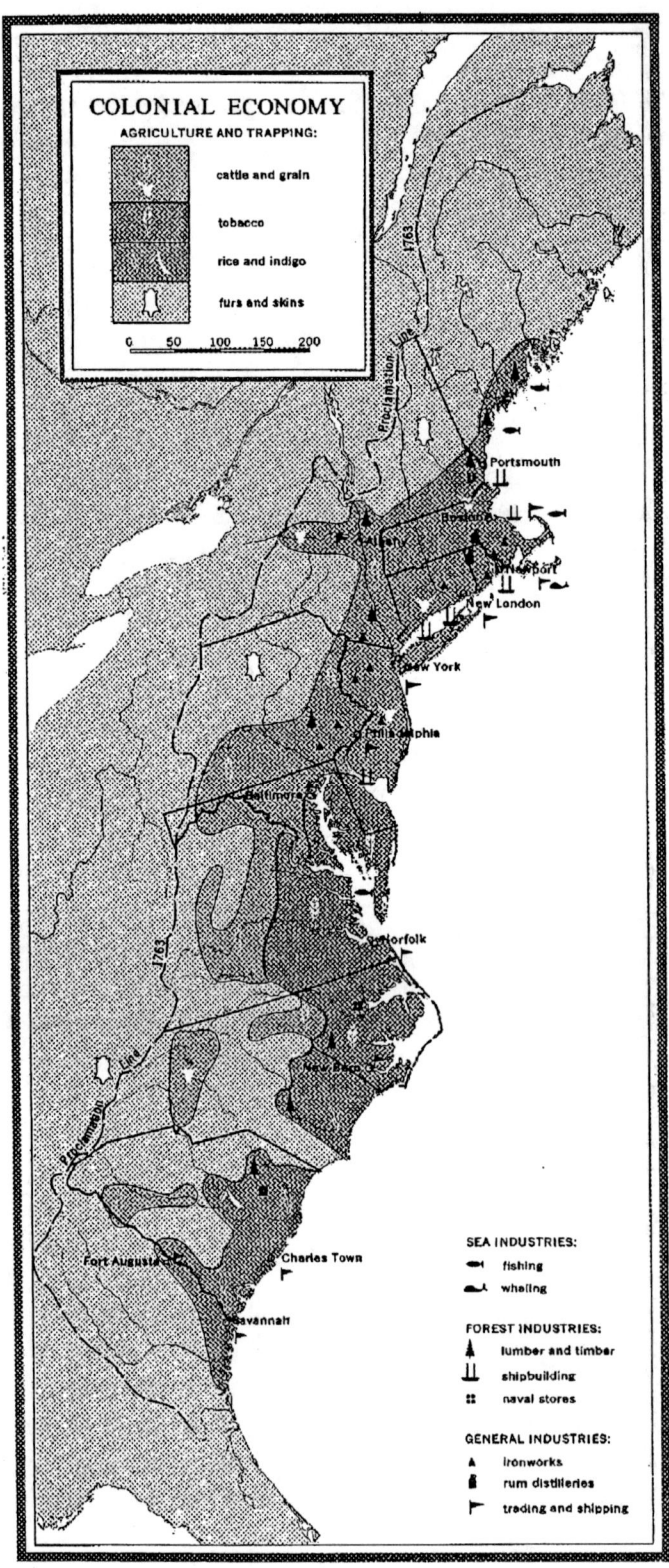

Based on National Origins and Religion Map, in *American Heritage Pictorial Atlas of United States History*, edited by Hilde Heun Kagan (N.Y.: American Heritage Publishing Co., 1966), 87.

© COPYRIGHT, The Center for Learning. Used with permission. Not for resale.

Advanced Placement U.S. History 1
Lesson 1
Handout 1 (page 4)

Name_____
Date_____

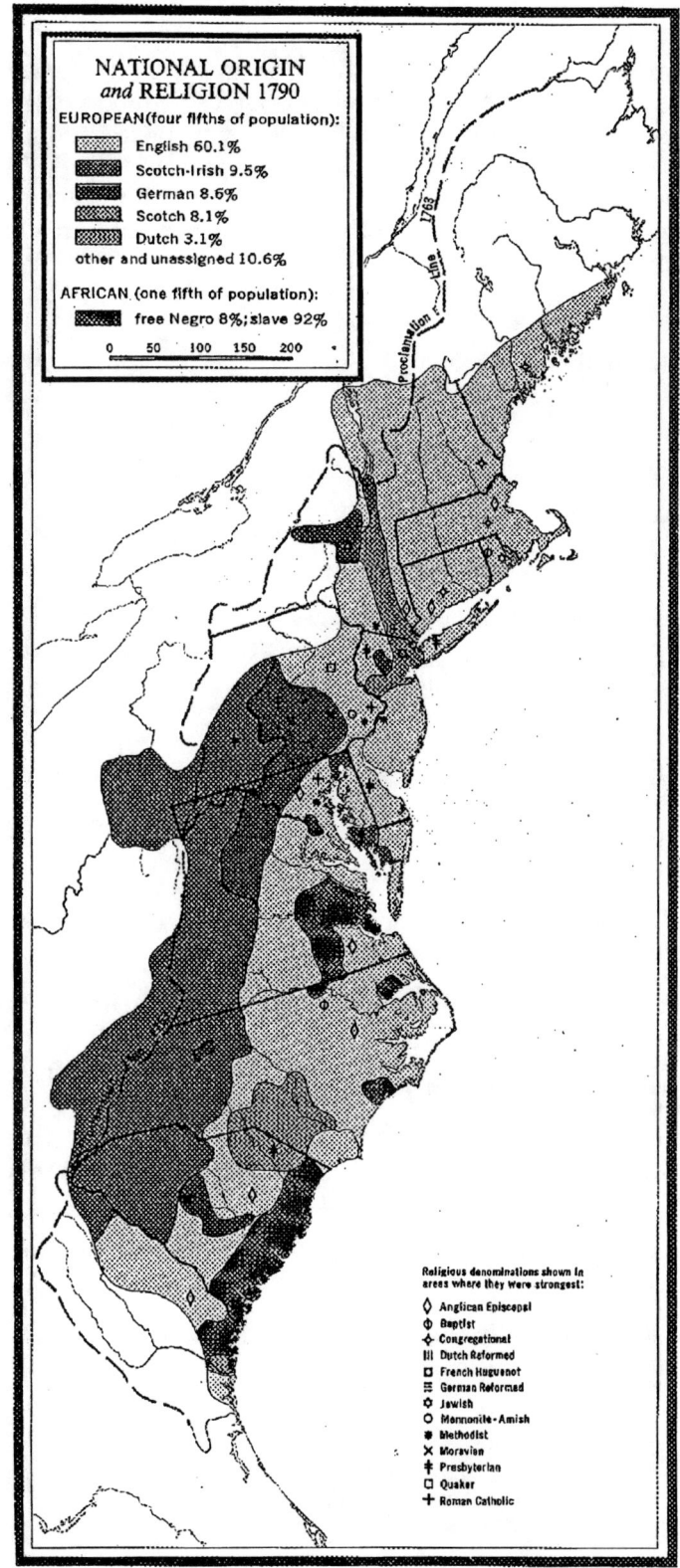

Ibid., 88.

Advanced Placement U.S. History 1
Lesson 2
Handout 2 (page 1)

Name_____
Date_____

From Authority to Individualism

The philosophies of Puritanism, the Great Awakening, and the Enlightenment provide much of the intellectual foundation for the establishment of the United States. Listed below are a series of key ideas of these three major intellectual trends. After you have studied these lists of ideas, assume each of the following roles: a Puritan farmer in Massachusetts in 1640; a Baptist seaman in Rhode Island in 1740; and a scholar of the Enlightenment at the College of William and Mary in Virginia in 1765. Compose paragraphs that characterize the thinking of each of these men on each of the points listed below:

   a. his concept of God

   b. the individual's reason for existence

   c. the individual's relationship to the church

   d. the need for education

   e. the individual's role in government

   f. the individual's responsibility for improving society

You will want to outline your answers on each of these points before you write your paragraphs. These paragraphs should prepare you for a class discussion on the contributions of each of these philosophies to the political development of the nation.

Notes on Puritanism

- The church formed the foundation of the Puritan social order.

- In God's plan of creation, all individuals were born with original sin; God predestined some people, the Elect, for salvation.

- Puritans had a strong sense of the sovereignty of God and the depravity of humanity. They strived hard to live in accordance with God's will.

- People were innately unequal, and only the saints could run the church and the elite, the government.

- Church membership was a prerequisite for participation in politics.

- Puritans came to America specifically to create a model "City upon a Hill," a Puritan utopia in the wilderness. It was thus appropriate to guard, warn, and reprove each other against moral lapses.

- The Puritans had a covenant, or contract, with God. If they kept the contract, God would grant them saving grace.

- Puritans believed it followed logically that civil government stems from a voluntary agreement by all church followers.

- In the distribution of communal lands, Puritans allotted acreage to individuals based on family size, need, and skills valued by the community.

- Everyone was legally required to attend church services.

© COPYRIGHT, The Center for Learning. Used with permission. Not for resale.

- Since the Scripture offered solutions to all problems of individual conduct, church and secular government, and social organization, and educated citizenry was necessary to enable individuals to interpret the meaning of the Scripture for their lives.

- Adherence to the strict Puritan moral code was both a sign of salvation and a path to prosperity.

- Puritans believed strongly in the correctness of their views and stood ready to use the power of the state to enforce religious uniformity.

- Puritan parents had an obligation to repress their children's willfulness and teach them obedience to God and their parents.

Notes on the Great Awakening

- Puritan piety of the seventeenth century had eroded by the eighteenth century in the New World atmosphere of individualism, optimism, and enterprise.

- Away from the persecutions in England, and removed by time and distance, Americans gave preference to the counting house over the meeting house.

- The Great Awakening was, in part, an emotional effort to reassert the earlier extreme piety over the rationalism and optimism of the Enlightenment.

- A heart open to the Divine Spirit was more important than a highly trained intellect.

- Revival preachers suggested that salvation was open to all who appealed to God, and they accused conservative clergymen of spiritual coldness.

- Most Americans had moved too far into modernity to share, even in times of religious revival, Jonathan Edwards's vision of the beauty and fitness of God's sovereignty and sinful humanity's helpless dependence on the miracle of Divine Grace.

- In America, with so many religious sects existing side by side, some people doubted whether any denomination had a monopoly over truth and grace.

- Most Congregationalist ministers in Massachusetts denounced the revivalists for permitting uneducated men to take it upon themselves to be preachers of the word of God and thus create confusion and errors and lead members away from their regular church.

- The widely-preached doctrine of salvation for all—of equal opportunity to share in God's grace—encouraged the notion of equal rights to share also in the good life on earth.

Advanced Placement U.S. History 1
Lesson 2
Handout 2 (page 3)

Name_____
Date_____

Notes on the Enlightenment

- The eighteenth-century Enlightenment produced a new climate of thought in which people believed that God had created humans and their world and that God had endowed humans with powers of observation and reason.

- People could observe this world and, by applying reason, could extract the "natural laws" that governed the phenomena.

- People were capable of perfecting human society by applying the rules of reason and removing human-created obstacles to a harmonious society.

- John Locke maintained that natural law ordained a government resting on the consent of the governed and respecting the inherent "natural rights" of all.

- God had created the world but had left the world to function according to the laws of nature.

- Man could perfect his world by finding the obstacles, removing them, and allowing the "natural laws" to operate freely.

- Men of the Enlightenment viewed the universe as a great clock, created by God, but allowed to operate freely. Thus, the object of the Enlightenment was to liberate the "natural laws," that would then apply themselves equally and thus create a new order with harmony and balance.

- God—the "Watchmaker"—was no longer present. One could not communicate with Him.

- Reason became the new "faith," and man became the new "god."

- Any unnatural laws, such as the mercantile regulations, conflicted with "natural laws" and had to be removed to have a perfectly functioning economy.

Advanced Placement U.S. History 1
Lesson 3
Handout 3 (page 1)

Name_____
Date_____

Colonial Exploitation—A Matter of Perception

Part A.

Use the documents below as a resource in responding to statements at the end. Mark each statement true or false, and list evidence from the readings that supports your response.

The Rights of Englishmen: Virginia, 1705

And also be it enacted, by the authority aforesaid, and it is hereby enacted, That all masters and owners of servants, shall find and provide for their servants, wholesome and competent diet, clothing, and lodging, by the discretion of the county court; and shall not, at any time, give immoderate correction; neither shall, at any time, whip a Christian white servant naked, without an order from a justice of the peace: And if any, notwithstanding this act, shall presume to whip a Christian white servant naked, without such order, the person so offending, shall forfeit and pay for the same, forty shillings sterling, to the party injured: To be recovered, with costs, upon petition, without the formal process of an action. . . .[1]

From W.W. Hening, *The Statutes at Large;
Being a Collection of All the Laws of Virginia*, 1823.

Political Control in Massachusetts, 1721

Although the government of this province be nominally in the Crown, and the governor appointed by your Majesty, yet the unequal balance of their constitution having lodged too great a power in the assembly, this province is, and is always likely to continue in great disorder. They do not pay a due regard to your Majesty's instructions. They do not make a suitable provision for the maintenance of their governor, and on all occasions they affect too great an independence on their mother kingdom. . . . An act of assembly . . . has not a little contributed to the present disorders there, inasmuch as by the said act it is provided, that no person shall be capable of representing any town or borough where such person is not a freeholder and settled inhabitant; from whence it happens, that the assembly is generally filled with people of small fortunes and mean capacities, who are easily led into any measures that seem to enlarge their liberties and privileges.[2]

Board of Trade to the king

The Propriety of Colonial Subordination, a British View, 1726

It is plain that none of the English plantations in America can with any reason or good sense pretend to claim an absolute legislative power within themselves. They cannot be possessed of any rightful capacity to contradict or evade the true intent and force of any Act of Parliament wherewith the wisdom of Great Britain may think fit to affect them from time to time. In discoursing on their legislative powers (improperly so called in a dependent government) we are to consider them only as so many corporations at a distance, invested with an ability to make temporary by-laws for themselves agreeable, but no ways interfering with the legal prerogative of the Crown, or the true legislative power of the mother state.[3]

A Short Discourse on the Present State of the Colonies

[1] John M. Blum, et. al., *The National Experience*, Vol. 1 (New York: Harcourt Brace Jovanovich, 1977), 54.
[2] Oscar Handlin, *A History of the United States*, Vol. 1 (New York: Holt, Rinehart and Winston, 1967), 153.
[3] Oscar Handlin, *A History of the United States*, 151.

© COPYRIGHT, The Center for Learning. Used with permission. Not for resale.

Another reason that the average lifespan was so short in Virginia is that—unlike New England—the colony included a large indentured servant class who were worked so hard by exploitative masters that it sent them to an early grave. About forty percent of those who immigrated to Virginia under indentures around the middle of the seventeenth century died before they had completed their four-year terms. Their masters were determined to get rich quick, and could see that driving servants mercilessly was the way to wealth. Back in England, centuries of tradition placed restraints on the length of the workweek and the intensity of labor that could be demanded from a bound servant, and selling servants against their will was forbidden. Traditional constraints did not operate on the other side of the ocean. On the isolated tobacco plantations there was no one to whom an overworked and abused young bondsman or bondswoman could appeal, and nothing to prevent them from being bought and sold like cattle. Masters pinched for other resources sometimes put up their servants as stakes in card games.[4]

And if any slave resists his master, or owner, or other person, by his or her order, correcting such slave, and shall happen to be killed in such correction, it shall not be accounted a felony; but the master, owner, and every such other person so giving correction, shall be free and acquit of all punishment and accusation for the same, as if such accident had never happened; And also, if any negro, mulatto, or Indian, bond or free, shall at any time, lift his or her hand, in opposition against any Christian, not being negro, mulatto, or Indian, he or she so offending, shall, for every such offence, proved by the oath of the party, receive on his or her bare back, thirty lashes, well laid on, cognizable by a justice of the peace for that county wherein such offence shall be committed.[5]

Hening, *Laws of Virginia*, 1823

The aims of the Virginia Company would have been more easily attained if the English had been able to put the local Indians to work as the Spaniards had. They tried, but were unsuccessful. The English knew something of the unhappy fate of the native peoples under Spanish rule, and claimed that they would be far more kind and benevolent. Their basic objectives, however, were no less exploitative. They assumed that the natives of North America would hand over their gold and silver, as well as food, and could doubtless be induced to produce more in exchange for the blessings of Christianity. As an anonymous poet of the day put it:

> The land full rich, the people easilie wonne,
> Whose gaines shall be the knowelage of our faith
> And our such ritches as the country hath.

. . . What could not be gained through compulsion might have been obtained through inducement. The English had things the Indians wanted and vice versa. Iron pots, knives, and fishhooks could be traded for corn, meat, fish, and fur. Some friendly trade did take place in the early years. John Rolfe's famous 1614 marriage to Powhatan's daughter, Pocahontas, symbolized the possibility of peaceful coexistence and eventual blending of the races. Very few Englishmen followed Rolfe's example, however. The fact that Pocahontas died two years later of a white man's disease contracted while on a trip to England was a better symbol of what was to happen. The Spanish, on the other hand, although not without prejudice, frequently intermarried with

---

[4] Stephan Thernstrom, *A History of the American People*, Vol. 1 (San Diego, California: Harcourt Brace Jovanovich, 1984), 29.

[5] Stephan Thernstrom, *A History of the American People*, Vol. 1, 67.

the natives, producing a large racially mixed *mestizo* element in the population. The English, by contrast, kept their distance despite the acute shortage of white women in the colony. They were aloof and imperious. Convinced of their moral as well as military superiority, they were unable to treat the natives with respect and understanding. Instead of asking, they demanded; if refused, they took anyway. When Powhatan sent them a message that struck them as "prowde and disdayneful," they launched a punitive expedition against a small tribe nearby, killing a dozen warriors and burning the village to the ground. After bringing the queen and her children back as captives, they thought better of it. The queen was put to the sword; the children they threw into the river, "shoteinge owtt their Braynes in the water."[6]

Braintree, 31 March, 1776

. . . I long to hear that you have declared an independency. And, by the way, in the new code of laws which I suppose it will be necessary for you to make, I desire you would remember the ladies and be more generous and favorable to them than your ancestors. Do not put such unlimited power into the hands of the husbands. Remember, all men would be tyrants if they could. If particular care and attention is not paid to the ladies, we are determined to foment a rebellion, and will not hold ourselves bound by any laws in which we have no voice or representation.

That your sex are naturally tyrannical is a truth so thoroughly established as to admit of no dispute; but such of you as wish to be happy willingly give up the harsh title of master for the more tender and endearing one of friend. Why, then, not put it out of the power of the vicious and the lawless to use us with cruelty and indignity with impunity? Men of sense in all ages abhor those customs which treat us only as the [servants] of your sex; regard us then as being placed by Providence under your protection, and in imitation of the Supreme Being make use of that power only for our happiness.[7]

---

[6] Stephan Thernstrom, *A History of the American People*, Vol. 1, 23–24.
[7] Beth Milstein Kava and Jeanne Bodin, *We, the American Women*, rev. ed. (Chicago: Science Research Associates, 1983), 38–39.

Advanced Placement U.S. History 1
Lesson 3
Handout 3 (page 4)

Name_____
Date_____

Respond *T* for true or *F* for false to the following statements. Be prepared to justify your decisions.

_____ 1. The English assumed their own superiority over the Spanish.

_____ 2. The British managed a better working relationship with the Native Americans than did the Spanish.

_____ 3. Tradition accorded the same rights to all classes in England and the colonies.

_____ 4. Indentured servants in Virginia had a legal status not accorded to African Americans.

_____ 5. The laws of colonial America presumed that "all men are created equal."

_____ 6. The British government viewed the thirteen American colonies as subordinate to the Crown.

_____ 7. The American colonies assumed their right to all the privileges accorded to Englishmen in the mother country.

_____ 8. From an Englishman's point of view, a little property does not an aristocrat make!

_____ 9. Women enjoyed greater equality in colonial America than they do today.

Part B.

In your group, assume one of the following roles: an indentured servant, slave, Native American, colonial planter, member of the British Board of Trade, or Abigail Adams. Prepare for a Meeting of the Minds role playing activity by outlining your position on each of the following questions:

a. How do you define *exploitation*?

b. Whose authority do you personally feel bound to obey? Why?

c. What one question would you like to ask another panelist to suggest evidence of his or her inconsistency or hypocrisy on this subject?

© COPYRIGHT, The Center for Learning. Used with permission. Not for resale.

Advanced Placement U.S. History 1
Lesson 3
Handout 3 (page 5)

Name_____
Date_____

Part C.

To conclude this lesson, write one paragraph describing a typical colonial planter's views on equality. Use specific examples from the documents or your Meeting of the Minds panel discussion to illustrate inconsistencies between his attitudes toward the mother country and his treatment of individuals within his own colony.

Advanced Placement U.S. History 1
Lesson 4
Handout 4 (page 1)

Name_____
Date_____

Democracy in Colonial Wethersfield, Connecticut

The following activity is designed to introduce you to document-based questions of the kind required on Advanced Placement examinations. For homework, read the documents on colonial Wethersfield, Connecticut. Before you begin, fold a piece of notebook paper into fourths and label each portion with one of the categories of evidence required to answer the question posed before Document A. As you read, jot down notes in the appropriate place on your chart indicating evidence related to the question. In front of each piece of evidence, put a + (plus) if the note suggests a step toward greater democracy, and a - (minus) if it suggests a trend away from democracy. *After each note, write, in parentheses, the letter of the document where you found the evidence.* On the back of the sheet, write down questions you have about specific documents.

Was American society, as evidenced by Wethersfield, Connecticut, becoming more "democratic" in the period from the 1750s to the 1780s? Discuss with reference to property distribution, social structure, politics, and religion.

Document A

Approximate population distribution of Wethersfield Village in 1756 and 1774.

	1756	1774
Whites	1,120	1,727
Free Blacks	40	62
Slaves	40	35

Document B

Approximate distribution of taxable property in Wethersfield Village in 1756 and 1773

Adult White Males Ranked in Deciles According to Value of Assessed Property	Average Tax Assessment of Property in Pounds Sterling (£)		Per Cent of Total Value of Assessed Property	
	1756	1773	1756	1773
Highest 10%	£127	£163	35.0	50.9
2nd 10%	71	65	19.5	20.4
3rd 10%	57	35	15.7	10.9
4th 10%	45	24	12.4	7.5
5th 10%	29	16	8.0	5.0
6th 10%	20	11	5.6	3.5
7th 10%	10	5	2.6	1.5
8th 10%	3	1	1.0	.2
9th 10%	1	0	.1	.0
Lowest 10%	0	0	.0	.0

Based on a representative sample of 100 adult white males.

© COPYRIGHT, The Center for Learning. Used with permission. Not for resale.

Advanced Placement U.S. History 1
Lesson 4
Handout 4 (page 2)

Document C

Distribution of land holdings in Wethersfield Village in 1756 and 1773.

Number of Acres in Holding	Per Cent of Total Land Holdings	
	1756	1773
1,000 or more	0	2
200–999	2	2
100–199	3	11
50–99	13	12
10–49	42	19
1–9	23	21
no land	17	33

Document D

Wealthiest adult white males in Wetherfield Village and their assessments in 1756 and 1774.

Year	Name	Assessment in Pounds Sterling (£)
1756	John Chester, Sr.	£320
	Thomas Belden	300
	Ebenezer Belden	290
	Josiah Grizwold	213
	Samuel Buck	188
1774	John Chester, Jr.	491
	Ebenezer Belden	323
	Josiah Buck	231
	Thomas Belden	217
	Silas Deane	208

Based on a representative sample of 100 adult white males.

Advanced Placement U.S. History 1
Lesson 4
Handout 4 (page 3)

Document E

Note: The pictures below are modern photographs of Wetherfield Village houses built between 1750 and 1775. The name of the original owner and the original owner's tax assessment on his total property (1775) are indicated.

Joseph Webb, £178

Charles Bulkley, £30

Thomas Harris, £52

Titus Buck, £17

© COPYRIGHT, The Center for Learning. Used with permission. Not for resale.

Document F

Reflecting on the conversations passed between us at Philadelphia, I am inclined to think that a number of inhabitants from this Colony [Connecticut] would venture on a settlement on the Ohio [River]. . . .[The Connecticut man's] first principle is to possess a disencumbered freehold, be it ever so small, in preference to the largest under quit rents and landlords. . . . The lands given should be divided into lots of about two or three hundred acres to each family and not more, for a Connecticut farmer with two hundred and fifty or three hundred acres of good land, is a rich man, that is, as rich as he wishes to be, for this Colony is now so full of inhabitants that there is not more than twelve acres to a person. . . .

I could procure a number [of settlers], sufficient for one town, who would incline to settle a little (or rather as much as possible), on the New England plan. . . . I will describe the method of settling and governing one of them, from which sample you will be acquainted with the whole. All lands in New England (except New Hampshire) are absolutely in the disposal of the General Assembly. . . . The Assembly grants on the following conditions: seventy families settle within such and such a time, four or five years perhaps. They, being settled, shall support a minister, or clergyman, of some of the protestant professions [i.e., denominations]. Dissenters [i.e. Congregationalists] to be preferred; also a school master. When they become more numerous and are desirous of it, they may send deputies to the general assembly, but when they do this and not before, they are liable to be taxed by the Assembly, for the support of the government. . . . All their domestic [concerns are] under their own regulation; they meet at least once in each year, and make choice of a number of the more steady of their number for selectmen, as they are called. These are officers . . . conducting all the public affairs of the town, in which they are accountable to no one but to the inhabitants in full meeting . . . their power expires within the year, when new ones [are chosen], or they are rechosen; they are in short a sort of censors on the manners of the people. They summon the people together as they judge proper. . . . Thus each town is in some degree a distinct republic with power even of passing what they call by-laws not repugnant to those of the Colony passed in General Assembly, where all are united by a representation chosen by each annually (or twice each year as is the case with us in Connecticut).

Silas Deane, Wethersfield merchant and a Connecticut delegate to the First Continental Congress, to Patrick Henry, a Virginia delegate to the First Continental Congress; written from Wethersfield, January 2, 1775.

Document G

Approximate Distribution of Adult White Males By Political Status in Wethersfield Village in the Periods 1751-1756 and 1771-1776

Political Status	Per Cent of Adult White Males	
	1751-1756	1771-1776
Able to meet freeman (voter) requirements	65	67
Taking freeman's oath (i.e. registering to vote)	40	62
Actually voting	30	53
Elected to all town offices (includes major offices, such as Selectmen and militia officers and minor offices such as jurors and surveyors)	32	52

Advanced Placement U.S. History 1
Lesson 4
Handout 4 (page 5)

Document H

Distribution of Major Town Offices among Assessed Adult White Males in Wethersfield Village in the Periods 1751–1756 and 1771–1776

Adult White Males Ranked in Deciles According to Value of Assessed Property	Per Cent of Adult White Males Elected to Major Town Office	
	1751–1756	1771–1776
Highest 10%	67	40
2nd 10%	15	37
3rd 10%	7	3
4th 10%	7	5
5th 10%	4	2
6th 10%	0	0
7th 10%	0	8
8th 10%	0	5
9th 10%	0	0
Lowest 10%	0	0

Document I

Note: The following letter was written by the Reverend Ebenezer Frothingham, a so-called Separatist minister, who had been jailed under Connecticut law for preaching in Wethersfield without the consent of the Reverend James Lockwood, the minister of the officially established Congregational Church in Wethersfield parish. Lockwood had initiated legal proceedings against Frothingham with the civil authorities.

> I [write] this by paper to Let you know this time perhaps you have a prejudice in your heart against me . . . [in] taking me from my Business that God in his providence Called me to . . . [Y]ou had no warrant from the word of God to do, nor authority under heaven—as a Civil authority has no Right to meddle with Ecclesiastical affairs (if I had transgress'd it was to the Church [to which] Christ the great sheperd has Committed all the power. . . .) Let me Intreat & warn you not to touch them [Separatists] in matters of Religion to Carry them before [civil] authority for in so doing you touch the apple of Christ's Eye, and these Lives will be a swift witness against you. . . .
>
> Reverend Ebenezer Frothingham, letter sent from the Hartford jail to the Reverend James Lockwood, minister of the First Church of Christ, Wethersfield,
> April 25, 1745

© COPYRIGHT, The Center for Learning. Used with permission. Not for resale.

Document J

In a civil community there is a necessary subordination of persons: some are entrusted with authority and power to rule over others, and to manage and conduct the public affairs: whilst others are in places of inferiority and subjection: and the health and prosperity of the community very much depends on the faithful discharge of the duties incumbent on the various members of it, resulting from the stations they hold in, or relations they bear to the state. . . .

As rulers are raised up by God, not for their own sakes, but for the people's; there is the highest reason they should be treated with respect, honour, and submission. For people to treat their persons or characters with rudeness and disrespect; to slight or vilify their laws or rashly censure their administrations; to cherish uneasy or mutinous dispositions, or give into seditious and riotous practices, is very inexcusable.

Reverend James Lockwood, minister of the First Church of Christ, Wethersfield; an Election Sermon preached before the Connecticut General Assembly, May 9, 1754

Document K

Note: The following two laws were enacted by the Connecticut Assembly in 1770.

. . . no person in this colony, professing the Christian protestant religion, who soberly and conscientiously dissent from the worship and ministry established by the laws of the colony and attend public worship by themselves, shall incur any of the penalties . . . for not attending the worship and ministry so established on the Lord's day or on account of their meeting together by themselves on said day for the public worship of God in a way agreeable to their consciences.

. . . all ministers of the Gospel that now are or hereafter shall be settled in this colony, during their continuance in the ministry, shall have all their estates . . . exempted out of the lists of polls [i.e., poll taxes] and rateable [i.e., assessable] estates.

Document L

The following is an account by Jared Ingersoll, a prominent New Haven attorney, of his detention in Wethersfield by a crowd of men who hoped to subvert the Stamp Act by forcing him to resign his position as distributor of stamps for Connecticut.

After some little Time, I dismounted and went into the House with the Persons who were called the Committee, the main Body continuing out doors. And here I ought not to omit mentioning that I was told repeatedly that they had no Intentions of hurting me or my Estate; but would use me like a Gentleman; this however I conclude they will understand was on condition I should comply with their demands. . . . This Committee behaved with Moderation and Civility, and I thought seemed inclined to listen to certain Proposals which I made, but when the Body of People came to hear them they rejected them, and nothing would do but I must resign [as distributor of stamps]. . . .

The Commandment [of the Committee] told me with seeming Concern in his Countenance that he could not keep the People off from me any longer; and that if they once began, he could not promise me where they would end. I now thought it was Time to submit. . . . Upon this I looked out at a front Window, beckoning the People and told them, I had consented to comply with their desires; and only waited to have something drawn up for me to sign. . . . Outside when I had done, a person who stood near me, told me to [shout] Liberty and Property, with three Cheers, which I did, throwing up my Hat into the Air; this was followed by loud Huzzas, and then many of the People were pleased to take me by the hand and tell me I was restored to their former Friendship. I then went with two or three more to a neighbouring House [Joseph Webb's house] where we dined.

Jared Ingersoll; account of "The Wethersfield Affair," Connecticut Gazette, September 27, 1765

Document M

To all Christian people believing in, and relying on that God to whom our Enemies have at last forced us to appeal, Be it known. . . . Driven to the last necessity and obliged to have recourse to arms, in defence of our Lives and our Liberties, and from the suddenness of the occasion deprived of that Legal Authority whose dictates we ever with pleasure obey, we find it necessary, for preventing disorders, irregularities and misunderstandings, in the course of our march and service, solemnly to agree to, and with each other, on the following Regulations and Orders, binding themselves by all that is dear and sacred, carefully and constantly to observe and keep them. . . .

So long as we continue in our present situation of a voluntary Independent Company, we engage to submit on all occasions to such decisions as shall be made and given by the majority of the officers we have chosen; and when any difference arises between man and man, it shall be laid before the officers aforesaid, and their decision shall be final. . . .

Scorning all ignoble motives, and superior to the low and slavish practice of enforcing on men their duty by blows, it is agreed, that when private admonition for any offence, by any of our Body committed, will not reform, public [warning] shall be made, and if that should not have the desired effect, after proper pains taken, and the same repeated, such incorrigible person shall be turned out of the Company as totally and unworthy of serving in so great and glorious a cause, and be delivered over to suffer the contempt of his Countrymen. . . .

In witness whereof, We have hereunto set our hands this 23 April, 1775.

Agreement of the Wethersfield Company of Volunteers under the command of Captain John Chester, Jr., April 23, 1775, signed by all volunteers prior to their engagement in the Battle of Bunker Hill

Document N

A stranger in the colony, upon hearing the inhabitants talk of religion, liberty, and justice, would be induced to believe that the Christian and civil virtues were their distinguishing characteristics; but he soon finds his mistake on fixing his abode among them. Their laws grind the poor, and their religion is to oppress the oppressed. The poll-tax is unjust and cruel. The poor man is compelled to pay [the poll tax], . . . work four days on the highways, serve in the militia four days, and pay three shillings for his hut without a window in it. The best house and richest man in the colony pays no more!

The law is pretended to exempt episcopalians, anabaptists, quakers, and others, from paying rates to the Sober Dissenters [i.e., Congregationalists]; but, at the same time, gives the Sober Dissenters power to tax them for minister, school, and town-rates, by a general vote; and no law or court can put asunder what the town has joined together.—The law also exempts [all members of other Christian churches who attend their own church] from paying to Sober Dissenters. . . . But, hence, if a man is sick, and does not attend more than 26 Sabbaths in a year, he becomes legally a Sober Dissenter. . . .

Reverend Samuel Peters, Anglican clergyman from England who visited much of Connecticut; *History of Connecticut*, 1782

Document O

How bless'd the sight of such a numerous train [people]
In such small limits, tasting every good
Of competence, of independence, peace,
And liberty unmingled; every house
On its own ground, and every happy swain [young man]
Beholding no superior, but the laws,
And such as virtue, knowledge, useful life,
And zeal, exerted for the public good,
Have rais'd above the throng. For here, in truth,
Not in pretence, man is esteem'd as man.
Not here how rich, of what peculiar blood,
Or office high; but of what genuine worth,
What talents bright and useful, what good deeds,
What piety to God, what love to man,
The question is.

. . .

      Beneath their eye,
And forming hand, in every hamlet, rose
The nurturing school; in every village, smil'd
The heav'n-inviting church, and every town
A world within itself, with order, peace,
And harmony, adjusted all its weal [well-being].

Timothy Dwight, prominent Connecticut poet and later President of Yale; "Greenfield Hill" (a poetic description of a typical Connecticut town), 1794

Advanced Placement U.S. History 1
Lesson 5
Handout 5 (page 1)

Name_____
Date_____

British Colonial Policy—A Tradition of Neglect

Assume that you are a French observer traveling in the American colonies in late 1763. On your return home, you expect to write a series of articles on the status of the American colonies in the British Empire. You will interview both a member of the Massachusetts legislature and the royal governor of New York. In doing background research for your interviews, you have listed several critical bits of information regarding both British and colonial developments. Your task now is to list, on your own paper, the six most perceptive questions you can formulate to ask *each* official. At the end, you will write a one-sentence conclusion showing why the recent British victory in the French and Indian Wars appears to foreshadow difficult times ahead in British-colonial relations.

Essential British Developments, 1607–1763

"Sir Robert Walpole, who became the king's chief minister in 1721, believed that it was to England's interest to let the colonies flourish without interference; and his policy of 'salutary neglect' continued until the 1760s."

Charles Sellers, Henry May, and Neil R. McMillen, *A Synopsis of American History*, Vol. 1, 3rd ed. (Chicago: Rand McNally College Publishing Company, 1974), 21.

"The English government wrongfully assumed that once the colonies were established, often without any help other than a written charter, they could be ignored much of the time. Most people in England had little interest in the colonies; the few who had direct dealings with settlers in the New World were merchants, concerned only with markets or raw materials."

Charles S. Miller and Natalie Joy Ward, *History of America*, Vol. 1 (New York: John Wiley and Sons, 1971), 94.

"The recent war (French and Indian War) had almost doubled the English national debt, which stood at £70,000,000 in 1756 and had risen to £130,000,000 in 1763. Taxpayers already grumbled at the rates and would certainly grumble more if asked to bear the total burden of imperial defense. Means would have to be found, it seemed to the ministers, to shift some of the expense to the colonists, who had also profited from the war and whom the garrisoned posts would protect."

Oscar Handlin, *The History of the United States*, Vol. 1 (New York: Holt, Rinehart, and Winston, 1967), 193.

"Neither Crown nor Parliament created much in the way of special machinery for colonial affairs, and for the most part regular executive agencies expanded their activities to include the colonies. Final authority over the colonies resided in the Privy Council, but the actual task of supervision was carried on by committees of the Council, regular agencies, and one specially constituted board (Board of Trade)."

Clinton Rossiter, *The First American Revolution* (New York: Harcourt, Brace & World, 1956), 106.

"The result of (this) conjunction of too much organization for detail and too little concern for unity—especially when intensified by distance, slowness of communication, inferiority of personnel, corruption, bribery, and colonial obstinacy—was a large measure of self-government for the colonies."

Rossiter, *First American Revolution*, 108.

© COPYRIGHT, The Center for Learning. Used with permission. Not for resale.

Advanced Placement U.S. History 1
Lesson 5
Handout 5 (page 2)

Name_____
Date_____

Essential Colonial Developments, 1607–1763

"Connecticut and Rhode Island, both founded without authority from the Crown, were granted royal charters of incorporation at the time of the Restoration. . . . In these two colonies, the pattern of self-government was most firmly established. Although the Crown retained considerable authority over their military, diplomatic, and commercial affairs, the extent of supervision was spotty and discontinuous."

Rossiter, *First American Revolution*, 103.

"By 1765, the assembly was dominant in almost every colony in continental America. The royal power of disallowance was still strong enough to prevent a complete overriding of the governor and other imperial officials, but shrewd observers were beginning to realize that only the full power of Parliament was now equal to the centrifugal practices of the assemblies."

Rossiter, *First American Revolution*, 117–118.

"In the old colonial system, a colony was to be a colony in the most obvious sense of the word: a perpetually subordinate agricultural and extractive area that served the mother country as a source of raw materials, a safety valve for excess or unwanted population, and a market for finished goods."

Rossiter, *First American Revolution*, 31.

"The key economic fact about colonial New England was that it was an area fitted by nature for commerce rather than agriculture. New Hampshire, Connecticut, Rhode Island, and Massachusetts formed the most unsatisfactory group of colonies, 'the most prejudicial Plantation to this Kingdom,' from the English point of view, for they produced no important staple for export."

Rossiter, *First American Revolution*, 40.

"Whatever the state of economic theory in colonial America, economic fact pointed toward the future. The long-run trend of the colonial economy was one of expansion—in population, productivity, capital accumulation, opportunity, social mobility, goals of enterprise, and openmindedness of economic thought."

Rossiter, *First American Revolution*, 39.

"The region lying between Albany and Baltimore supported the best-balanced economy in colonial America. Like New England a booming commercial area, it was far less dependent on circuitous trading to pile up remittances to England. . . . Toward the middle of the eighteenth century it took the lead from New England in the number and productivity of its manufacturing enterprises. Climate, soil, topography, and ingenuity combined to make the middle colonies, especially Pennsylvania, the soundest economic unit in the imperial structure."

Rossiter, *First American Revolution*, 45.

© COPYRIGHT, The Center for Learning. Used with permission. Not for resale.

Advanced Placement U.S. History 1
Lesson 5
Handout 5 (page 3)

Name_____
Date_____

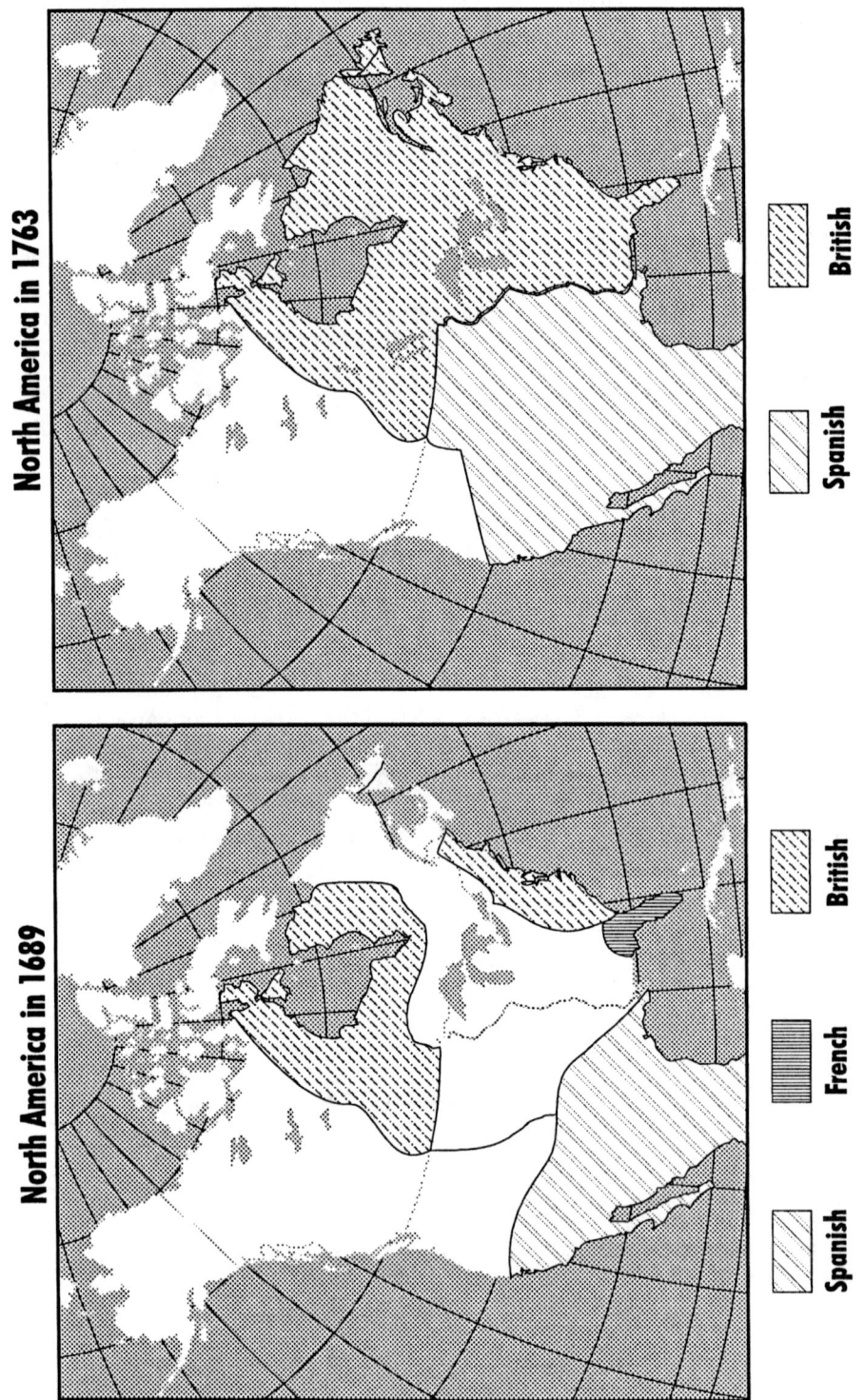

Advanced Placement U.S. History 1
Lesson 6
Handout 6

Name_____
Date_____

The Colonies by 1763—A New Society?

The writing assignment below will help you to fit together some of the ideas you have learned about colonial America and also to see how the sections of a well-organized essay relate to each other. It should prove to be a useful tool for reviewing for the Advanced Placement examination or a final examination in your history class.

Listed below in scrambled order are the thesis, the plan of attack, and four topic sentences for the paragraphs of the body of an essay on differences between the mother country and the American colonies in 1763. You should be able to determine the sequence of each of the sentences in a well-organized essay. A thesis defines the central argument in any essay. A plan of attack states the method of organization to be used in the paper. In this essay, the thesis and the plan of attack together form a simple introductory paragraph. You may wish to add transition words or phrases for greater clarity.

Using this foundation for the essay, complete the paper. Each paragraph of the body should include a clear description of the English practice, at least two specific facts explaining how the colonial practice differed from that of the mother country, and an attempt to account for the differences between England and the colonies. End the paper by writing an appropriate conclusion that summarizes your points and draws a logical conclusion about their significance for the future development of the country, in light of the British victory in the French and Indian War in 1763.

Scrambled Sentences

a. Changes in religion, economics, politics, and social structures illustrate this Americanization of the transplanted Europeans.

b. In a similar economic revolution, the colonies outgrew their mercantile relationship with the mother country and developed an expanding capitalist system on their own.

c. Building on English foundations of political liberty, the colonists extended the concepts of liberty and self-government far beyond those envisioned in the mother country.

d. Between the settlement at Jamestown in 1607 and the Treaty of Paris in 1763, the most important change that occurred in the colonies was the extension of British ideals far beyond the practice in England itself.

e. By 1763, although some colonies still maintained established churches, other colonies had accomplished a virtual revolution for religious toleration and separation of church and state.

f. In contrast to the well-defined and hereditary classes of England, the colonies developed a fluid class structure which enabled the industrious individual to rise on the social ladder.

© COPYRIGHT, The Center for Learning. Used with permission. Not for resale.

Part 2
Establishing the Nation

Part 2 analyzes the causes and effects of the American Revolution and the steps toward establishing a workable government to deal with domestic and foreign problems. It concludes with a lesson on the emerging culture and sense of national pride in the new nation. In studying this unit, you will learn how the colonies justified their rebellion and how they combined theory and experience in creating a new nation.

By the conclusion of the unit, you should be able to answer the following basic questions:

- What caused the American Revolution?

- How did the colonists justify declaring their independence from Great Britain?

- What political, economic, and social effects resulted from the American Revolution?

- Why did the Articles of Confederation fail to create a workable central government?

- How did the Founding Fathers balance competing interests in a way that calmed the fears of opponents of a strong central government?

- How did early leaders shape the foundations of American foreign policy?

- What caused the development of political parties during the Washington administration?

- How did decisions of the Marshall court strengthen the Supreme Court and the national government?

- How did Americans create a sense of unity and shared national identity in the early nineteenth century?

Advanced Placement U.S. History 1
Lesson 7
Handout 7 (page 1)

Name_____
Date_____

The Path to Revolution, 1763–1776

For homework, research the events leading to the American Revolution, and complete the chart. Start at the bottom to work toward the Revolution. Explain why both 1776 and 1763 were turning points in American history.

Part A.

Significance of 1776 as a Turning Point:

British action	Rationale	Colonial reaction	Rationale
Lexington and Concord		Paine's "Common Sense"	
Coercive or "Intolerable" Acts		boycott, convening First Contintental Congress	
Quartering Act 1774		protest in assemblies	
Tea Act		protest, Boston Tea Party, boycott	
Townshend duties		boycotts, petitions, newspaper attacks	

© COPYRIGHT, The Center for Learning. Used with permission. Not for resale.

Advanced Placement U.S. History 1
Lesson 7
Handout 7 (page 2)

Name_____
Date_____

British action	Rationale	Colonial reaction	Rationale
Repeal of Stamp Act and passage of Declaratory Act		rejoicing over repeal; ignoring Declaratory Act	
Stamp Act		petitions, boycott, violence	
Currency Act		smoldering resentment	
Sugar Act		Boston experimented with boycotts	
Proclamation of 1763		resentment and failure to comply	

© COPYRIGHT, The Center for Learning. Used with permission. Not for resale.

Advanced Placement U.S. History 1
Lesson 7
Handout 7 (page 3)

Name_____
Date_____

Part B.

Significance of 1763 as a Turning Point:

From your readings and your completed chart, answer the following questions:

1. "The Americans have made a discovery, or think they have made a discovery, that we mean to oppress them; we have made a discovery, or think we have made a discovery, that they intend to rise up in rebellion against us. We know not how to advance; they know not how to retreat." *Edmund Burke*[1]

    a. What kind of "advance" or adjustment might the British have made to halt the escalation of the colonial rebellion?

    b. What kind of retreat would the colonists have had to make to be acceptable to Britain?

2. How does your completed chart help to explain the lack of meaningful compromise between Britain and the colonies in the years between 1763 and 1776?

3. Was the dominant concern of the colonists economic or political? Explain your answer.

4. From your readings and your chart, what role do you believe each of the following played in producing wide-based support for independence in the colonies?

    a. Inept British officials, such as Charles Townshend or George Grenville

---

[1] Stephan Thernstrom, *A History of the American People*, Vol. 1 (New York: Harcourt Brace Jovanovich, 1984), 144.

Advanced Placement U.S. History 1
Lesson 7
Handout 7 (page 4)

    b. Dedicated radicals, such as Samuel Adams and Patrick Henry

    c. Responsible moderates, such as John Adams, Benjamin Franklin, and Thomas Jefferson

5. How did each of the following affect relations between the mother country and the colonies?

    a. Timing of new regulations

    b. Distance and lack of an easy means of communication

    c. Repeals of the Stamp Act and most Townshend duties

6. Now try to write your own one or two sentence thesis on the causes of the American Revolution.

Advanced Placement U.S. History 1
Lesson 8
Handout 8

Name_____
Date_____

The Declaration of Independence

For homework, read the Declaration of Independence and write answers to the following questions on your own paper.

1. What is the purpose of the Declaration of Independence as stated in the introductory paragraph?

2. What groups did the Continental Congress hope to sway by this document?

3. According to Jefferson, who has the right to create a government? According to Jefferson, what is the purpose of a government? According to Jefferson, what should be done if a government fails to fulfill its purpose?

4. Using your answers in item 3, summarize in your own words Jefferson's philosophy of government. (This philosophy is Jefferson's major premise or assumption in the Declaration of Independence.)

5. Select any five grievances against George III and the English government that Jefferson lists in the Declaration of Independence. Copy the grievance, and state for each one a British law or action which may have prompted that complaint.

6. What legal means of protest did the colonists take to convince the British to change their ways?

7. How did the British respond to these complaints?

8. What conclusion did Jefferson then draw?

9. What sacrifices were the signers willing to make to gain their independence?

© COPYRIGHT, The Center for Learning. Used with permission. Not for resale.

Advanced Placement U.S. History 1
Lesson 9
Handout 9 (page 1)

Name_____
Date_____

The Effects of the American Revolution

For homework, read the following selections from a monograph on effects of the American Revolution, and complete the outline at the end of the handout.

J. Franklin Jameson (1859–1937) served as managing editor of the *American Historical Review* from its founding in 1895 to 1928, except for a four-year interval. After a teaching career at Johns Hopkins, Brown University, and The University of Chicago, Jameson served as Director of Historical Research in the Carnegie Institution of Washington and as Chief of the Division of Manuscripts in the Library of Congress. Jameson's work, *The American Revolution Considered as a Social Movement*, stresses the extent of social reforms won at home during the war.

The Revolution as a Social Movement

It is indeed true that our Revolution was strikingly unlike that of France, and that most of those who originated it had no other than political programme, and would have considered its work done when political independence of Great Britain had been secured. But who can say to the waves of revolution: Thus far shall we go and no farther? The various fibres of a nation's life are knit together in great complexity. It is impossible to sever some without also loosening others, and setting them free to combine anew in widely different forms. The Americans were much more conservative than the French. But their political and their social systems, though both were, as the great orator said, still in the gristle and not yet hardened into the bone of manhood, were too intimately connected to permit that the one should remain unchanged while the other was radically altered. The stream of revolution, once started, could not be confined within narrow banks, but spread abroad upon the land. Many economic desires, many social aspirations were set free by the political struggle, many aspects of colonial society profoundly altered by the forces thus let loose. The relations of social classes to each other, the institution of slavery, the system of landholding, the course of business, the forms and spirit of the intellectual and religious life, all felt the transforming hand of revolution, all emerged from under it in shapes advanced many degrees nearer to those we know . . .

If then it is rational to suppose that the American Revolution had some social consequences, what would they be likely to be? . . .

Allowance has to be made for one important fact in the natural history of revolutions, and that is that, as they progress, they tend to fall into the hands of men holding more and more advanced or extreme views, less and less restrained by traditional attachment to the old order of things. Therefore the social consequences of a revolution are not necessarily shaped by the conscious or unconscious desires of those who came into control of it at later stages of its development. . . .

All things considered, it seems clear that in most states the strength of the revolutionary party lay most largely in the plain people, as distinguished from the aristocracy. It lay not in the mob or rabble, for American society was overwhelmingly rural and not urban, and had no sufficient amount of mob or rabble to control the movement, but in the peasantry, substantial and energetic though poor, in the small farmers and frontiersmen. And so, although there were men of great possessions like George Washington and Charles Carroll of Carrollton who contributed a conservative element, in the main we must expect to see our social changes tending in the direction of levelling democracy.

© COPYRIGHT, The Center for Learning. Used with permission. Not for resale.

It would be aside from the declared purpose of these lectures to dwell upon the political effects which resulted from the victory of a party constituted in the manner that has been described. There are, however, some political changes that almost inevitably bring social changes in their wake. Take, for instance, the expansion of the suffrage. The status in which the electoral franchise was left at the end of the Revolutionary period fell far short of complete democracy. Yet during the years we are considering the right of suffrage was much extended. The freeholder, or owner of real estate, was given special privileges in four of the new state constitutions, two others widened the suffrage to include all owners of either land or personal property to a certain limit, and two others conferred it upon all tax-payers. Now if . . . we are considering especially the status of persons, we must take account of the fact that the elevation of whole classes of people to the status of voters elevates them also in their social status. . . .

A far more serious question, in any consideration of the effect of the American Revolution of the status of persons, is that of its influence on the institutions of slavery, for at this time the contrast between American freedom and American slavery comes out, for the first time, with startling distinctness. It has often been asked: How could men who were engaged in a great and inspiring struggle for liberty fail to perceive the inconsistency between their professions and endeavors in that contest and their actions with respect to their bondmen? How could they fail to see the application of their doctrines respecting the rights of man to the black men who were held among them in bondage far more reprehensible than that to which they indignantly proclaimed themselves to have been subjected by the King of Great Britain? . . .

There is no lack of evidence that, in the American world of that time, the analogy between freedom for whites and freedom for blacks was seen. If we are to select but one example of such evidence, the foremost place must surely be given to the striking language of Patrick Henry, used in 1773, when he was immersed in the struggle against Great Britain. It is found in a letter which he wrote to one who had sent him a copy of Anthony Benezet's book on slavery.

It is not amazing [he says] that at a time, when the rights of humanity are defined and understood with precision, in a country above all others fond of liberty, that in such an age and in such a country we find men professing a religion the most humane, mild, gentle and generous adopting a principle as repugnant to humanity as it is inconsistent with the Bible and destructive to liberty? . . . Would anyone believe I am the master of slaves of my own purchase? I am drawn along by the general inconvenience of living here without them. I will not, I can not justify it. However culpable my conduct, I will so far pay my devoir to virtue, as to own the excellence and rectitude of her precepts, and lament my want of conformity to them. I believe a time will come when an opportunity will be offered to abolish this lamentable evil. . . .

Along with many examples and expressions of individual opinion, we may note the organized efforts toward the removal or alleviation of slavery manifested in the creation of a whole group of societies for these purposes. The first anti-slavery society in this or any other country was formed on April 14, 1775, five days before the battle of Lexington, by a meeting at the Sun Tavern, on Second Street in Philadelphia. The members were mostly of the Society of Friends.

... The New York "Society for Promoting the Manumission of Slaves" was organized in 1785, with John Jay for its first president. In 1788 a society similar to these two was founded in Delaware, and within four years there were other such in Rhode Island, Connecticut, New Jersey, Maryland, and Virginia; and local societies enough to make at least thirteen, mostly in the slave-holding states.

In actual results of the growing sentiment, we may note, first of all, the checking of the importation of slaves, and thus the horrors of the trans-Atlantic slave trade. The Continental Congress of 1774 had been in session but a few days when they decreed an "American Association," or non-importation agreement, in which one section read: "That we will neither import nor purchase any slave imported after the first day of December next, after which we will wholly discontinue the slave trade, and will neither be concerned in it ourselves, nor will we hire our vessels nor sell our commodities or manufactures to those who are concerned in it"; and the evidence seems to be that the terms of this agreement were enforced throughout the war with little evasion.

Still further, the states in which slaves were few proceeded, directly as a consequence of the Revolutionary movement, to effect the immediate or gradual abolition of slavery itself. Vermont had never recognized its existence, but Vermont was not recognized as a state. Pennsylvania in 1780 provided for gradual abolition, by an act which declared that no negro born after that date should be held in any sort of bondage after he became twenty-eight years old, and that up to that time his service should be simply like that of an indented servant or apprentice. Now what says the preamble of this act? That when we consider our deliverance from the abhorrent condition to which Great Britain had tried to reduce us, we are called on to manifest the sincerity of our professions of freedom, and to give substantial proof of gratitude, by extending a portion of our freedom to others, who, though of a different color, are the work of the same Almighty hand. Evidently here also the leaven of the Revolution was working as a prime cause in this philanthropic endeavor.

The Superior Court of Massachusetts declared that slavery had been abolished in that state by the mere declaration of its constitution that "all men are born free and equal." In 1784 Connecticut and Rhode Island passed acts which gradually extinguished slavery. In other states, ameliorations of the law respecting slaves were effected even though the abolition of slavery could not be brought about. Thus in 1782 Virginia passed an act which provided that any owner might, by an instrument properly attested, freely manumit all his slaves, if he gave security that their maintenance should not become a public charge. It may seem but a slight thing, this law making private manumission easy where before it had been difficult. But it appears to have led in eight years to the freeing of more than ten thousand slaves, twice as great a number as were freed by reason of the Massachusetts constitution, and as many as there were in Rhode Island and Connecticut together when the war broke out. . . .

Thus in many ways the successful struggle for the independence of the United States affected the character of American society by altering the status of persons. The freeing of the community led not unnaturally to the freeing of the individual; the raining of colonies to the position of independent states brought with it the promotion of many a man to a higher order in the scale of privilege or consequence. So far at any rate as this aspect of life in America is concerned, it is vain to think of the Revolution as solely a series of political or military events. . . .

Advanced Placement U.S. History 1
Lesson 9
Handout 9 (page 4)

If anything should occur which should administer a great shock to the entire social system of the country, it would dislodge and shake off from the body politic, as an outworn vesture, such institutions as no longer met our needs. Now this is just what the Revolution did. It broke up so much that was traditional and customary with the Americans, in dissolving their allegiance to a monarchy for which they had felt a most loyal attachment, that whatever else was outgrown or exotic seemed to be thrown into the melting-pot, to be recast into a form better suited to the work which the new nation had before it. . . .

But in a quiet, sober, Anglo-Saxon way a great change was effected in the land-system of America between the years 1775 and 1795.

In the first place, royal restrictions on the acquisition of land fell into abeyance. The king's proclamation of 1763, forbidding settlement and the patenting of lands beyond the Alleghenies, and those provisions of the Quebec Act of 1774 which in a similar sense restricted westward expansion and the formation of new, interior colonies had, it is true, never been executed with complete rigidity, but they. and the uncertainties of the months preceding the war, had certainly checked many a project of large colonization and many a plan for speculation in land. Now these checks were removed. Moreover, all the vast domains of the Crown fell into the hands of the states, and were at the disposal of the state legislatures, and it was certain that these popular assemblies would dispose of them in some manner that would be agreeable to popular desires. Whether the land law in respect to old holdings should be altered by the Revolution or should remain unchanged, it was certain that in respect to new lands, on which the future hopes of American agriculture and settlement rested, a more democratic system would be installed.

Then there was the matter of quit-rents, which in most of the colonies, according to the terms on which lands were granted to individual occupants, were to be paid to the crown or to the proprietary of the province. They ranged from a penny an acre to a shilling a hundred acres per annum. It is true that payment was largely evaded, but since the amount received at the time when the Revolution broke out was nearly $100,000, we may count the quit-rent as something of a limitation upon the ready acquisition of land. So at any rate the colonists regarded it, for in making their new constitutions and regulations respecting lands they abolished quit-rents with great emphasis and vigor, and forbade them for the future.

Another encumbrance on land-tenure which the Revolution removed was the provision, by British statute intended to ensure an adequate supply of masts for the royal navy, that no man should cut white-pine trees on his land till the king's surveyor of woods had surveyed it and designated the trees, sometimes many in number, which were to be reserved for the king's use. . . .

With the coming of the Revolution, the restriction came to an end, and fee simple was fee simple.

In the fourth place, great confiscations of Tory estates were carried out by the state legislatures, generally in the height of the war. New Hampshire confiscated twenty-eight estates, including the large property of its governor, Sir John Wentworth. In Massachusetts a sweeping act confiscated at one blow all the property of all who had fought against the United States or had even retired into places under British authority without permission from the American government. . . .

© COPYRIGHT, The Center for Learning. Used with permission. Not for resale.

Advanced Placement U.S. History 1
Lesson 9
Handout 9 (page 5)

Name_____
Date_____

The largest estate confiscated was that of the Penn family, proprietaries of Pennsylvania, which they estimated at nearly a million pounds sterling. The commissioners of the state of Maryland who sold confiscated property in that state took more than £450,000 sterling. . . .

In one colony and another, hundreds of estates were confiscated. Altogether, it is evident that a great deal of land changed hands, and that the confiscation of Tory estates contributed powerfully to break up the system of large landed properties, since the states usually sold the lands thus acquired in much smaller parcels. . . .

If, as I have suggested, nothing was more important in the American social system than its relation to the land, and if the Revolution had any social effects at all, we should expect to see it over-throwing any old-fashioned features which still continued to exist in the land laws. What, then, was the old land-law in the American colonies? The feudal ages had discovered that, if men desired to give stability to society by keeping property in the hands of the same families generation after generation, the best way to do this was to entail the lands strictly, so that the holder could not sell them or even give them away, and to have a law of primogeniture, which, in case the father made no will, would turn over all his lands to the eldest son, to the exclusion of all the other children. There could not be two better devices for forming and maintaining a land-holding aristocracy. When the Revolution broke out, Pennsylvania and Maryland had abolished primogeniture, and South Carolina had abolished entails. But in New York, New Jersey, Virginia, North Carolina, and Georgia, entails and primogeniture flourished almost as they did in old England. Indeed, Virginian entails were much stricter than the English. The New England colonies had a peculiar rule of their own for the descent of land in case a man left no will. They liked a democratic distribution, and yet they could not feel quite comfortable to cut away entirely from the old English notions about the eldest son. Moreover, their Puritanical feelings for the law of Moses (Deut. xxi 17) was very strong. Accordingly, they arranged that in such a case all the children should inherit equally, except that the eldest son should have a double share. Then came the Revolution. In ten years from the Declaration of Independence every state had abolished entails excepting two, and those were two in which entails were rare. In fifteen years every state, without exception, abolished primogeniture and in some form provided for equality of inheritance, since which time the American eldest son has never been a privileged character. It is painful to have to confess that two states, North Carolina and New Jersey, did not at once put the daughters of the Revolution upon a level with the sons. North Carolina for a few years provided for equal distribution of the lands among the sons alone, and not among daughters save in case there were no sons. New Jersey gave the sons a double share. But elsewhere absolute equality was introduced. Now I submit that this was not an accident. How hard Washington found it to get these thirteen legislatures to act together! And yet here we find them all with one accord making precisely the same changes in their landlaws. Such uniformity must have had a common cause, and where shall we find it if we do not admit that our Revolution, however much it differed from the French Revolution in spirit, yet carried in itself the seeds of a social revolution?[3]

---

[3] Jameson, J. Franklin, *The American Revolution Considered as a Social Movement* (Princeton, N.J.: Princeton University Press, 1926), 9–38 passim.

© COPYRIGHT, The Center for Learning. Used with permission. Not for resale.

Advanced Placement U.S. History 1
Lesson 9
Handout 9 (page 6)

Name_____
Date_____

1. List questions you have about the reading.

2. To what extent does available information about the author help you to understand his perspective, or point of view?

3. After reading the article, what questions might you ask that would suggest a different thesis?

Title:

Author:

Date of publication:

Author's thesis:

Author's evidence:

a.

b.

c.

d.

e.

Author's conclusion about the significance of the topic:

Write a paragraph in your own words explaining the gist of the article, the nature of evidence, and the significance of the topic.

Advanced Placement U.S. History 1
Lesson 10
Handout 10

Name_____
Date_____

The Articles of Confederation—The Challenge of Sovereignty

Listed below are a series of facts about the Articles of Confederation. First, explain the significance of each term. Then, examine the list, divide the items into three or four categories, and label the categories. Finally, write a thematic sentence that states or implies a relationship among the categories and the lesson title.

Facts about the Articles of Confederation

a. No separate executive
b. Northwest Ordinances of 1785 and 1787
c. One vote per state
d. No federal courts
e. Shays' Rebellion
f. British retention of forts in Northwest
g. No regulation of interstate commerce
h. Boundary disputes between states
i. No power to tax
j. States taxed each other's goods
k. Kept the states together
l. Treaty of Paris, 1783
m. Federal aid to education (Northwest Ordinance, 1785)
n. No national currency
o. Members often failed to attend Congress
p. Inability to protect settlers from Indians
q. Barbary pirates raided shipping
r. Inability to repay French loans
s. Spain's denial of right of deposit at New Orleans
t. Little trade with Britain

Categories

Write here your organizing sentence to state or imply a relationship among the categories you developed above and the lesson title.

© COPYRIGHT, The Center for Learning. Used with permission. Not for resale.

Advanced Placement U.S. History 1
Lesson 11
Handout 11 (page 1)

Name_____
Date_____

The Constitution—Balancing Competing Interests

Part A.

Americans' experience with British rule and the Articles of Confederation gave rise to considerable apprehension about the placement of power in a new government. The Founding Fathers attempted to allay those fears through compromises that safeguarded the interests of competing groups. The following chart lists some of those fears. Research the Constitution and related sources to identify the cause of each fear and how one or more provisions of the Constitution calmed that fear. Your completed chart should enable you to understand part B on the conflicting view of later historians about the motives of the Founding Fathers.

Fear	Source of fear	Provision to calm the fear
Fear of large states		
Fear of the people		
Fear of weak central government		
Fear of central government		
Fear of unwritten word		
Fear of other states		
Fear of foreign powers		
Fear of strong executive		
Fear of losing individual rights		

© COPYRIGHT, The Center for Learning. Used with permission. Not for resale.

Advanced Placement U.S. History 1 Name_____
Lesson 11 Date_____
Handout 11 (page 2)

Part B.

Study the following readings in preparation for a discussion about motives of the Founding Fathers in writing the Constitution.

> The *Progressive point of view* was most ably expressed in Charles A. Beard's book, *An Economic Interpretation of the Constitution*, published in 1913. Although other scholars—historians like Richard Hildreth and John Marshall and political scientists like J. Allen Smith—had taken an economic approach to the Constitution, none had been able to demonstrate as convincingly as Beard that the document might be best interpreted in economic terms. The key to Beard's pathbreaking study was a person-by-person examination of the economic holdings and status of the framers of the Constitution. Using the Treasury Records, Beard was able to show that most of these men held public securities—a form of personal property which would obviously increase in value if a new Constitution were written to strengthen the government and improve the credit standing of the country. His research showed also that these men had heavy investments in three other kinds of personal property. Beard's findings led him to conclude, "The movement for the Constitution of the United States was originated and carried through principally by four groups of personalty interests which had been adversely affected under the Articles of Confederation: money, public securities, manufactures, and trade and shipping." His implication was clear: the framers had designed the Constitution to safeguard the kind of property in which they had a pocketbook interest.
>
> If the lower class represented a majority of the population, how could personal propertyholders who were a minority control the Constitutional Convention? Beard's answer to this question rested mainly upon his interpretation of the property qualifications for voting. Most small farmers and workingmen, according to him, were in debt or owned so little property that they could not qualify for voting rights. "A large propertyless mass was, under the prevailing suffrage qualifications, excluded at the outset from participation . . . in the work of framing the Constitution." Thus Beard viewed the Constitution as an undemocratic document foisted upon the majority of the American people by a propertied minority.
>
> When it came to ratifying the Constitution, the "propertyless masses," according to Beard, were excluded once again from political participation. Only one-fourth of the adult white men in the nation voted on the question of ratification, because the rest were either disfranchised or disinterested. The total number voting in favor of the Constitution came to no more than one-sixth of the adult white males. Those who supported ratification on the state level, Beard wrote, had precisely the same economic interests as the framers of the document. In his eyes the voting on ratification, like the framing of the Constitution itself, gave clear evidence of a class conflict: the struggle pitted men with substantial personal property on the one hand against small farmers and debtors on the other.
>
> Gerald N. Grob and George A. Billias, eds., *Interpretations of American History*, Vol. 1, 3rd ed. (New York: Free Press, 1978), 150–151.

Advanced Placement U.S. History 1
Lesson 11
Handout 11 (page 3)

There is little doubt that the Anti-federalists would have won a Gallup poll.
. . .

In this situation, however, the Federalists were the realists. They had learned from experience that the natural rights philosophy, taken straight, would go to a nation's head and make it totter or fall. . . .

Federalists believed that the slogans of 1776 were outmoded; that America needed integration, not state rights; that the immediate peril was not tyranny, but disorder or dissolution; that certain political processes, such as war, foreign affairs, and commerce, were national by nature; that the right to tax was essential to any government; and that powers wrested from king and parliament should not be divided among thirteen states, if the American government was to have any influence in the world.

Samuel E. Morison and Henry S. Commager, *The Growth of the American Republic*, 5th ed (New York: Oxford Univ., 1962), I, 290.[1]

---

[1] Quoted from Bernard Feder, ed. *Viewpoints: USA* (New York: American Book Company, 1967), 62.

Advanced Placement U.S. History 1
Lesson 12
Handout 12 (page 1)

Name_____
Date_____

Foundations of American Foreign Policy

Part A.

For homework, complete the following matching exercise. Write the letter of the foreign policy on the line by the item which best matches the description. Then list the events by name in their chronological order.

Description

_____ 1. Spain guaranteed American farmers the use of the Mississippi River and the right of deposit in New Orleans in an attempt to prevent an Anglo-American reproachment.

_____ 2. Restored the status quo ante-bellum when a lengthy war and protracted negotiations failed to produce a victory for either side

_____ 3. United States stopped all foreign trade in an effort to pressure Britain and France into respecting our rights as a neutral.

_____ 4. United States would refrain from intervention in European affairs but would regard as an "unfriendly act" any attempt at further colonization in the Western Hemisphere.

_____ 5. Britain agreed to evacuate forts in the Northwest but made no concessions on impressment or violations of our rights as a neutral.

_____ 6. United States staunchly rejected French demands for an apology, a loan, and a bribe as a condition of negotiations.

_____ 7. United States declared war against Britain in an effort to gain Canada, an end to Indian troubles on the frontier, and respect for our rights as a neutral.

_____ 8. Spain ceded Florida to the United States and renounced any claim to Oregon in return for a United States renunciation of any tenuous claims we might have to Texas and $5 million in claims of Americans against the Spanish government in Florida.

_____ 9. Britain and the United States agreed to mutual disarmament of the Great Lakes.

_____ 10. United States would remain friendly and impartial toward both Britain and France rather than become embroiled in the French Revolution in the critical first years of the Republic.

_____ 11. United States purchased a huge amount of land in order to guarantee Americans permanent use of the Mississippi River.

_____ 12. Americans might sign commercial treaties with foreign nations but should steer clear of permanent alliances that might entangle this country in European conflicts.

Foreign Policy	**Chronological Order**
a. Adams–Onis Treaty	1.
b. Proclamation of Neutrality	2.
c. Monroe Doctrine	3.
d. Rush-Bagot Treaty	4.
e. Pinckney Treaty	5.
f. XYZ Affair	6.
g. Washington's Farewell Address	7.
h. Louisiana Purchase	8.
i. Treaty of Ghent	9.
j. Jay Treaty	10.
k. Embargo	11.
l. War of 1812	12.

© COPYRIGHT, The Center for Learning. Used with permission. Not for resale.

Advanced Placement U.S. History 1　　　　　　　　　　　Name_____
Lesson 12　　　　　　　　　　　　　　　　　　　　　　　Date_____
Handout 12 (page 2)

Part B.

John Quincy Adams has been called the most effective secretary of state in our nation's history. He served in that position during the Monroe administration (1817–1825) just prior to assuming the presidency himself. Perhaps one reason for his success was having a clear notion of what American foreign policy was at the time and where it should be headed. Assume the role of Secretary Adams as he prepared a report on the state of American foreign policy for his incoming secretary of state, Henry Clay, at the beginning of 1825.

In this report, include the following:

1. A succinct statement of United States foreign policy at the time

2. A statement of his philosophy on the national interests/morality issue as a guide to policy determination

3. What he had achieved as secretary of state and how it had benefited the nation

4. His vision of two critical foreign policy goals for the future

Advanced Placement U.S. History 1　　　　　　　　Name_____
Lesson 13　　　　　　　　　　　　　　　　　　　　Date_____
Handout 13 (page 1)

The Development of Political Parties

Part A.

For homework, complete part A of this handout. Study the following statements on the philosophies of Alexander Hamilton and Thomas Jefferson. Your teacher will assign you the role of either Alexander Hamilton, Secretary of the Treasury, or Thomas Jefferson, Secretary of State. Write the name of your role at the top of the chart that follows. You are to do appropriate research in preparation for a Cabinet meeting with President Washington tomorrow. The agenda includes discussion of the following issues:

a. Funding the foreign, national, and state debt

b. Proposed Bank of the United States

c. Whiskey excise

d. Protective tariff

e. The country's appropriate response to the French Revolution

You must be ready to present your position on each issue and explain your rationale consistent with your philosophy of government. Use the accompanying chart to organize your research.

Hamilton

Alexander Hamilton, born in the West Indies in 1757, came to the colonies to go to school and, later, to attend King's College (Columbia University). At seventeen, he composed a series of persuasive letters to the editor on the principles involved in the colonial dispute against the mother country. When war broke out, Hamilton earned a commission as a captain in a New York artillery company. After serving a short time in Washington's army, Washington appointed him to be his aide and to think for him, as well as execute orders. After a time, Hamilton retired to study law and serve as receiver of Continental taxes for New York, a position which soon taught him the desirability of a strong national government capable of enforcing its will on adamant states' rights advocates. In 1786, at the poorly-attended Annapolis Convention, Hamilton introduced a resolution to call a convention of all thirteen states to consider revisions to the Articles of Confederation. At the resulting Philadelphia Convention in 1787, Hamilton used all of his influence to push for the strongest possible central government. He later helped to pen a series of "Federalist Papers," designed to build support for the new government. When the Constitution went into effect, Washington again chose Hamilton to do his thinking, this time in organizing the Department of the Treasury to put the nation on a sound financial footing.

In that capacity, Hamilton, now married to the aristocratic Betsy Schuyler of New York, displayed his elitist tendencies and his lack of faith in the common people. Hamilton believed in the development of a strong central government and the development of a self-sufficient economy based on industry as well as agriculture. Although he had strongly supported the American Revolution, he favored the Tory government of Britain over the revolutionary government of France. In creating a financial policy for the new nation, Hamilton aimed, specifically, to establish the credit of the nation, build a strong central government, consolidate the support of the wealthy for the new government, and help to solve the currency shortage that threatened the development of industry in the United States.

© COPYRIGHT, The Center for Learning. Used with permission. Not for resale.

Advanced Placement U.S. History 1
Lesson 13
Handout 13 (page 2)

Name_____
Date_____

Jefferson

Thomas Jefferson, the elder son of a prominent Virginia planter, inherited two farms in 1757 when he was fourteen. Jefferson, who had been educated by local tutors, developed an insatiable appetite for learning. Leaving his plantations in the hands of overseers, he moved to Williamsburg at seventeen to pursue professional training at the College of William and Mary. There, young Jefferson became acquainted with the ideas of the Enlightenment and accepted the belief of enlightened thinkers in the capacity of man to solve problems of society. He agreed, too, with the English philosopher, John Locke, that man has certain natural rights that government has an obligation to protect; if the government fails to protect those rights to life, liberty, and property, the people have a right to alter or abolish their government. This idea of the social contract became a major premise of the Declaration of Independence. Jefferson's reading ranged widely in politics, philosophy, religion, natural science, music, architecture, sculpture and painting, the law, literature, and agriculture. Serving in the Virginia colonial legislature in the critical years beginning in 1769, Jefferson soon had ample evidence to convince him of the undesirability of an authoritarian government like that of Britain. He quickly concluded that government should be restricted to protecting the natural rights of all men. Jefferson's tenure as Minister to France just before the French Revolution reinforced that view. The same concern for human rights prompted Jefferson to withhold support for the new Constitution until the framers agreed to the addition of a Bill of Rights.

While he was not a systematic thinker, Jefferson had clarified his thinking on the proper role of government by the time he agreed to serve as Secretary of State in the Washington administration. He wanted the states to retain as much authority as possible and the powers of the national government interpreted narrowly. He had seen enough of the manufacturing centers of Europe to be assured that an agricultural economy should avoid many of the undesirable consequences of industrialization and urbanization. Although he favored nonintervention in European affairs as a way of preserving peace, he, nonetheless, strongly favored the French against the British in foreign matters.

© COPYRIGHT, The Center for Learning. Used with permission. Not for resale.

Advanced Placement U.S. History 1
Lesson 13
Handout 13 (page 3)

Name_____
Date_____

Your Role_____

Issue	Your position	Justification for your position
Funding Debts		
Bank of the United States		
Whiskey Excise		
Protective Tariff		
Response to French Revolution		

Advanced Placement U.S. History 1 Name_____
Lesson 13 Date_____
Handout 13 (page 4)

Part B.

After the class presentation on the role-playing activity, answer the questions below.

1. What was the most persuasive argument presented by the opposition on each of the following issues?

    a. Funding national, state, and local debts

    b. Bank of the United States

    c. Whiskey excise

    d. Protective tariff

    e. Response to the French Revolution

2. What is your greatest concern regarding the overall philosophy of the opposition?

3. What, in your view, would be the greatest service your own philosophy could make to the future welfare of the country?

4. How did the disagreement between Hamilton and Jefferson lead to the development of political parties?

Advanced Placement U.S. History 1
Lesson 14
Handout 14 (page 1)

Name_____
Date_____

The Role of the Judiciary in the Creation of the National State

Part A.

Listed below are nine important events in the life of John Marshall. Explain the significance of each factor in shaping his political philosophy.

1. John Marshall served in the Revolutionary Army for four years and suffered through Valley Forge with George Washington, whom he adored.

2. John Marshall served in the Virginia legislature (1783–89) when Virginia planters refused to pay their debts to English merchants.

3. Daniel Shays led his rebellion, and this country experienced a depression as well as European disrespect during the period Marshall served in the Virginia legislature.

4. The bloody tales of the French Revolution filtered across the Atlantic to America. Many Americans believed that the situation in France had become chaotic.

5. President Washington had been attacked because of the Proclamation of Neutrality in 1793, his actions to suppress the Whiskey Rebellion, and his acceptance of the unpopular Jay Treaty.

© COPYRIGHT, The Center for Learning. Used with permission. Not for resale.

Advanced Placement U.S. History 1
Lesson 14
Handout 14 (page 2)

Name_____
Date_____

6. John Marshall was sent to France in the late 1790s to try to stop French raids on American shipping. Talleyrand tried to bribe Marshall and the other American representatives. Marshall also saw Napoleon emerging from the chaos of the French Revolution. He feared this autocratic new leader.

7. Thomas Jefferson and James Madison wrote the Kentucky and Virginia Resolutions, which were debated during the period 1799–1800. (One state declared a law of Congress unconstitutional, another state declared the same law void, a third state said the law was invalid, a fourth state said it was valid, and some states denied the right of Congress to pass the law and asserted the states' right to disregard the law.)

8. John Adams appointed John Marshall to serve as Chief Justice of the Supreme Court.

9. Thomas Jefferson, a Republican, became president, and Republicans took control of Congress.

Part B.

The following are four major cases of the Marshall court:

Marbury v. Madison (1803)

McCulloch v. Maryland (1819)

Dartmouth College v. Woodward (1819)

Gibbons v. Ogden (1824)

Research each case in order to explain the following points:

- What was the case?
- What was the decision of the Supreme Court?
- What was the reasoning of the Supreme Court?
- What long-range significance did the case have in American history?

© COPYRIGHT, The Center for Learning. Used with permission. Not for resale.

Advanced Placement U.S. History 1 Name_____
Lesson 14 Date_____
Handout 14 (page 3)

Part C.

Read the following statement and cite evidence from this lesson to support the assessment of John Marshall.

> I do fully believe that if American law were to be represented by a single figure, skeptic and worshipper alike would agree without dispute that the figure would be one alone, and that one John Marshall.[1]
>
> —Oliver Wendell Holmes

---

[1] "John Marshall" by Stephen B. Presser in *The Guide to American Law: Everyone's Legal Encyclopedia*, *Vol. M* (St. Paul, Minn.: West Publishing Company, 1984), 278.

Advanced Placement U.S. History 1
Lesson 15
Handout 15 (page 1)

Name_____
Date_____

Coming Together—Nationalism Ascendant

Part A.

In his 1837 lecture entitled "The American Scholar," Ralph Waldo Emerson formulated the American "Intellectual Declaration of Independence": "We have listened too long to the courtly muses of Europe. We will walk on our own feet; we will work with our own hands; we will speak with our own minds."[1] This project will help you to pull together elements of emerging nationalism and interpret its significance as a turning point in national thought and action in the first half of the nineteenth century.

Section I: Political Developments

In a brief paragraph for each, explain how the following items contributed to a greater sense of independence and nationhood:

   a. Louisiana Purchase

   b. Embargo

   c. War of 1812

   d. John Marshall Supreme Court decisions

   1. *McCulloch v. Maryland*

   2. *Dartmouth College v. Woodward*

   3. *Gibbons v. Ogden*

   e. Adams-Onis Treaty

   f. Monroe Doctrine

Section II: Economic Developments

Create a visual to illustrate how enactment of Henry Clay's American System would help to unify New England, the South, and the West and create a self-sufficient, interdependent country. Be sure to give your poster an appropriate and descriptive title.

Section III: Cultural Developments

   a. *Art*: Find and photocopy at least two examples of each of following and write a brief statement beneath each grouping indicating how it illustrates the theme of nationalism.

   1. Hudson River School (Thomas Cole or Asher Durand, for example)

   2. Rocky Mountain School (Thomas Moran or Albert Bierstadt, for example)

   3. Genre artists (William Sydney Mount or John Quidor, for example)

   b. *Architecture*: Find and photocopy at least two examples of Thomas Jefferson's architecture (Monticello, University of Virginia, Virginia Capitol, for example) and beneath the pictures explain why Jefferson believed Classical Revival was a more appropriate style than Georgian for public buildings in the new United States.

---

[1] Lewis Mumford, ed., *Ralph Waldo Emerson: Essays and Journals* (Garden City, N.J.: Doubleday and Company, Inc., 1968), 47–48.

© COPYRIGHT, The Center for Learning. Used with permission. Not for resale.

Advanced Placement U.S. History 1
Lesson 15
Handout 15 (page 2)

Name_____
Date_____

    c. *Literature*: Select any three of the following writers, and for each one identify one of his writings, its theme, and how it illustrates the theme of your project.

      1. Ralph Waldo Emerson

      2. John Greenleaf Whittier

      3. Oliver Wendell Holmes

      4. Henry Wadsworth Longfellow

      5. Nathaniel Hawthorne

Your completed project will serve as a resource in your class discussion of emerging nationalism and its importance to the new nation.

Part B.

A political cartoon allows the creator to present an editorial view in pictures. To conclude this lesson, assume the role of either an American or a Continental cartoonist to create a political cartoon that conveys your perspective on the significance of the growing sense of national identity in the new American nation.

Part 3
Solidifying the American Nation-State

Part 3 considers the growth of industry and democracy and then proceeds to analyze social weaknesses of the country. The quest for Manifest Destiny and the agitation for social change tested the strength and nature of the Union. When compromise failed to resolve the nature of the Union, Civil War resulted. Although the war finalized the political nature of the Union, it did not resolve lingering social problems.

By the conclusion of the unit, you should be able to answer the following basic questions:

- What factor led to the development of industry in America after the War of 1812?

- How and why did early American factories avoid the evils of British industry?

- How did Jacksonian Democracy differ from Jeffersonian Democracy?

- How did social reformers in the ante-bellum period propose to improve American society?

- To what extent was the Mexican War in the national interest?

- How did the continental expansion promote both nationalism and sectionalism?

- How did the Compromises of 1820, 1833, and 1850 delay the Civil War?

- To what extent were individuals rather than events responsible for abolition?

- How is Reconstruction interpreted differently by conservatives and liberals?

Advanced Placement U.S. History 1
Lesson 16
Handout 16 (page 1)

Name_____
Date_____

The End of Homespun—The Early Industrial Revolution

Part A.

Read the documents below, and, on your own paper, compile a list of factors that contributed to the development of the early Industrial Revolution in the United States.

Document A

The Congress shall have power to promote the progress of science and useful arts, by securing for limited times to authors and inventors the exclusive right to their respective writings and discoveries.

Constitution, Article I, Section 8.8

Document B

The Erie Canal's . . . impact on the entire American economy was enormously stimulating. In the pre-Civil War years state governments supplied about three-quarters of the total funds invested in canals, and roughly half of the capital used to construct the rail network. Local communities and counties were also extremely active in subsidizing transportation improvements. In some cases, like that of the Erie Canal, these developmental efforts were operated as well as financed by governments. It was more common, however, for new ventures to be launched with government funds raised by taxation or the sale of public securities, then placed under private control. Public policy reflected not only widespread confidence in private enterprise, but a determination that it needed spurring to carry out large-scale development projects.

Government actively promoted industrial growth in other ways: erecting tariffs to protect domestic manufacturers from foreign competition; creating new legal arrangements, like the corporation, to stimulate the release of economic energy; and building schools to produce a better educated labor force.

Stephan Thernstrom, *A History of the American People*,
Vol. 1 (New York: Harcourt Brace Jovanovich, 1984), 217.

Document C
A New England Farm Family's Reasons for Moving to a Mill Town, 1843

You will probely want to know the cause of our moveing here. One of them is the hard times to get a liveing off the farm for so large a famely. So we have devided our famely for the year. We have left Plummer and Luther to care for the farm with granmarm and Aunt Polly. The rest of us have moved to Nashvill thinking the girls and Charles they would probely worke in the Mill. But we have had bad luck in giting them in. Only Jane has got in yet. Ann has the promis of going to the mill next week. Hannah is going to school. We are in hopes to take a few borders but have not got any yet.

Letter by Jemima W. Sanborn to Richard and Ruth Bennett, Nashua, New Hampshire, May 14, 1843. Quoted in Gary Kulik, Roger Parks, and Theodore Z. Penn, eds. *The New England Mill Village, 1790–1860* (Cambridge, Mass.: The MIT Press, 982), 397.

© COPYRIGHT, The Center for Learning. Used with permission. Not for resale.

Document D

The first postwar Congress, one of the most fruitful of the nineteenth century, took long strides toward Clay's goal of an American System. By 1816 the Republican party numbered in its ranks a large cluster of interest groups, both urban and rural clamoring for protective duties on certain foreign goods entering the American market. Leading the protectionists were those who had invested in New England textile mills and Pennsylvania iron-smelters when the embargo and war had choked off European supplies. Seconding them were the hemp-growers of Kentucky, the wool-growers of Ohio and Vermont, and an assortment of Southerners and Westerners who hoped either to promote industry or to expand their domestic market behind a tariff wall.

The cries of the protectionists grew louder when British exporters, seeking to dispose of surpluses accumulated during the war and to drive competing American manufacturers out of business, flooded the American market with relatively low-priced goods. A member of Parliament suggested that British goods might even be sold at a loss for a time, in order "to stifle in the cradle, those rising manufactures in the United States, which war has forced into existence, contrary to the natural course of things." In the critical years immediately following the war, British competition forced many small, less efficient American manufacturers to close their doors. Protectionists claimed that the British were plotting to wreck the American economy and asserted that a higher tariff was essential for national economic survival. America's "infant industries" were fragile things, they said, requiring the tender care of the federal government while they matured.

John H. Blum et al., The National Experience, Part I
(New York: Harcourt Brace Jovanovich, 1977), 180.

Document E

Principal Canals in 1840

Note that canals mainly facilitated east-west traffic, especially along the great Lake Erie artery. No comparable network of canals existed in the South—a disparity that helps to explain Northern superiority in the Civil War that came two decades later.

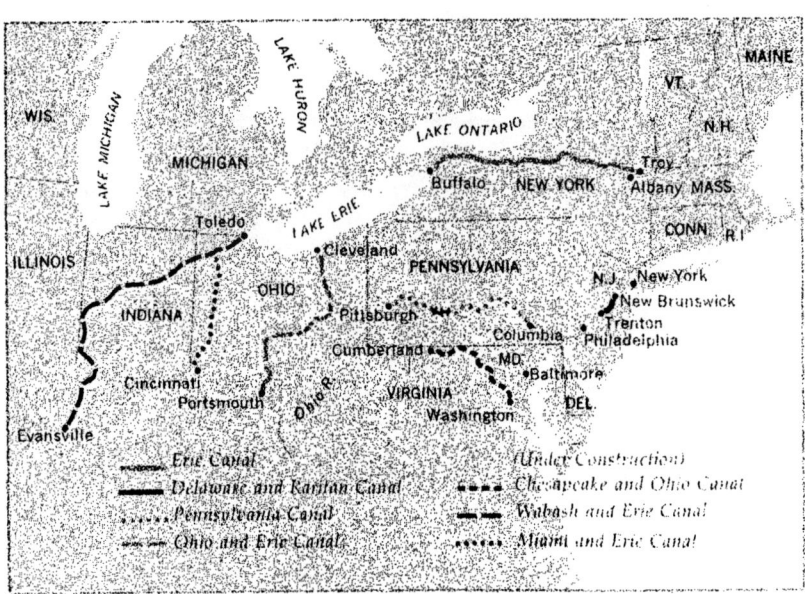

Thomas A. Bailey and David M. Kennedy, *The American Pageant*, 7th ed. (Lexington, Mass.: D.C. Heath, 1983), 286.

Document F

Eli Whitney, Samuel Slater, Oliver Evans, and others furnished the necessary technology for industry. In 1793, Eli Whitney developed a system of interchangeable parts which greatly accelerated the process of assembly. Samuel Slater, in 1790, brought the plans for a cotton mill by memory from England. Later, in 1804, Oliver Evans developed a high-pressure steam engine which was applied to mills and printing presses. Evans also experimented with techniques of mass production, which he employed in a flour mill.

Document G

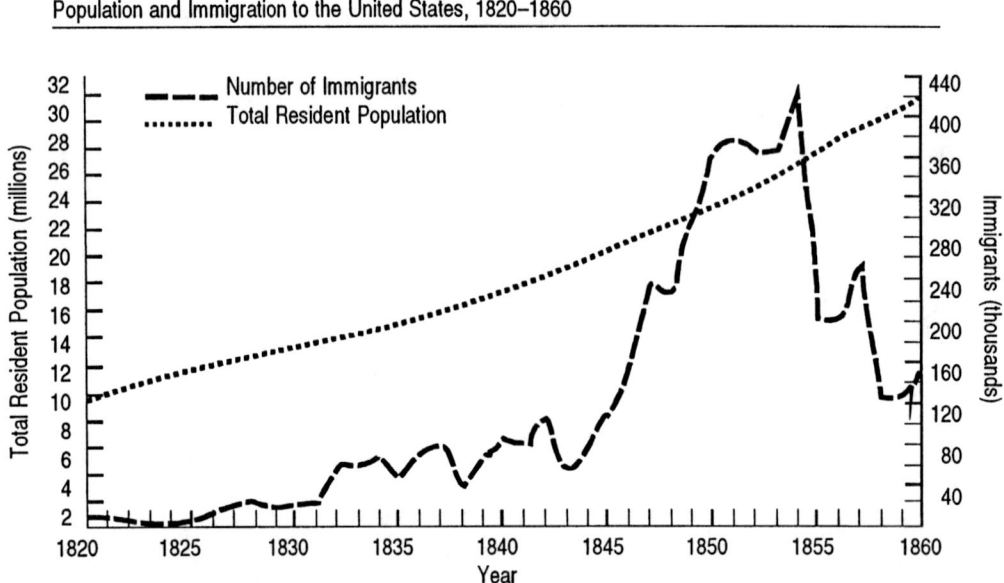

Source: Historical Statistics of the United States, Colonial Times to 1957

Fig. 16.2. Irwin Unger, *These United States, Vol. 1* (Boston, Mass.: Little Brown and Company, 1978), 237.

Document H

The federal judiciary also promoted business enterprise. In *Gibbons v. Ogden (1824)*, the Supreme Court overturned a New York state law that had given Robert Fulton and Robert Livingston a monopoly when Chief Justice Marshall ruled that the trade fell under the sway of the commerce clause of the Constitution. Thus Congress, not New York, had the controlling power. Since the federal government issued such licenses on a nonexclusive basis, the decision ended monopolies on waterways throughout the nation. Within a year, 43 steamboats were plying Ogden's route.

In defining interstate commerce broadly, the Marshall Court expanded federal powers over the economy while limiting the ability of states to control economic activity within their borders. Its action was consistent with its earlier decision in *Dartmouth College v. Woodward (1819)*, which protected the sanctity of contracts against interference by the states.

"If business is to prosper," Marshall wrote, "men must have assurance that contracts will be enforced."

Mary Beth Norton, et al., *A People and a Nation, Vol. I* (Boston, Mass.: Houghton Mifflin, 1982), 223.

Advanced Placement U.S. History 1
Lesson 16
Handout 16 (page 4)

Name_____
Date_____

Document I

Investment capital for the early factory system came from both the public and private sectors. Commercial capitalists who could not invest in commercial enterprises during the Embargo and War of 1812 found an opportunity to put their money into early factories in the United States. State governments, and, to a far lesser degree, the federal government, invested in canals, banks, railroads and manufacturing firms to promote the economy of the area.

Document J

The Bank of the United States, which had not been rechartered in 1811, had closed its doors. Without a national bank it was doubly difficult for the nation to pay for the war. Instead of being able to borrow from one central bank, the government had to deal with many. Without any Bank of the United States, state banks (private banks chartered by the states) had multiplied rapidly, each issuing its own paper money. There was no one national currency. In the dark days of the war, after the British burned Washington, many holders of these state bank notes tried to convert them to gold and silver (specie) as the banks had promised. But, lacking specie, the banks refused. As a result the value of the state bank notes declined. The bonds of the federal government sold below face value, and the national debt soared.

To deal with these hard economic problems, the federal government decided to charter a bank similar to Hamilton's bank of 1791, but with a larger capital. Again the government would hold one-fifth of the stock and would name one-fifth of the directors. Southern statesmen who had argued against the constitutionality of the old bank now suddenly changed their tune. They favored the second Bank of the United States. Madison, who had called Hamilton's bank unconstitutional, signed the new bank bill on April 10, 1816.

Daniel Boorstin and Brooks M. Kelley, *A History of the United States* (Lexington, Mass.: Ginn and Company, 1986), 170.

Part B.

Rank in order the factors on your list to assess their relative importance in promoting the early Industrial Revolution in the United States. Then, write a one-sentence thesis statement to account for the early development of manufacturing in this country.

© COPYRIGHT, The Center for Learning. Used with permission. Not for resale.

Advanced Placement U.S. History 1
Lesson 17
Handout 17 (page 1)

Name_____
Date_____

The Early Industrial Revolution—Maintaining a Sense of Community

Read the following documents and answer the questions at the end.

Document A

The new urban agglomerations were drab places, blackened with the heavy soot of the early coal age, settling alike on the mills and the workers' quarters, which were dark at best, for the climate of the Midlands is not sunny. Housing for workers was hastily built, closely packed, and always in short supply, as in all rapidly growing communities. Whole families lived in single rooms, and family life tended to disintegrate. A police officer in Glasgow observed that there were whole blocks of tenements in the city, each swarming with a thousand ragged children who had first names only, usually nicknames—like animals, as he put it. . . .

Hours in the factories were long, fourteen a day or occasionally more; and though such hours were familiar to persons who had worked on farms, or at domestic industry in rural households, they were more tedious and oppressive in the more regimented conditions that were necessary in the mills. Holidays were few, except for the unwelcome leisure of unemployment, which was a common scourge, because the short-run ups and downs of business were very erratic during this period of bewildering expansion. A day without work was a day producing nothing to live on, so that even where the daily wage was relatively attractive the worker's real income was chronically insufficient. Workers in the factories, as in the mines, were almost entirely unorganized. They were a mass of recently assembled humanity without traditions or common ties. Each bargained individually with his employer, who, usually a small businessman himself, facing a ferocious competition with others, often in debt for the equipment in his factory, or determined to save money in order to purchase more, held his "wages bill" to the lowest possible figure that he could manage.

R.R. Palmer and Joel Colton, *A History of the Modern World*, 5th ed. (New York: Alfred A. Knopf, 1978), 423–424.

Document B

Some village mill owners provided schools for children whom they employed. The first was Samuel Slater's Sunday School, established in Pawtucket in the 1790s as essentially a secular institution for teaching reading, writing, and arithmetic and modeled on similar English schools. Other mill owners convinced the local town to establish a district school nearby. Like rural schools that operated only during those times when children were not needed to help on the farm, mill village schools were in session only a few months a year.

To encourage social order and regular behavior, village mill proprietors often gave land to any religious denomination willing to organize and build a church. The Baptist Fiske family of Fiskdale, Massachusetts, went a step further and provided its workers with a church of the owners' choice . . .

The work force in cotton mill villages was ethnically homogeneous in the early nineteenth century. It consisted mainly of New Englanders of British extraction and some British immigrants. Beginning with Samuel Slater, British immigrants for many years provided a significant number of skilled workers required in textile manufacturing.

The overwhelming majority of production workers were native born and this would remain so until the late 1840s and the early 1850s.

Gary Kulik et al., eds. *The New England Mill Village, 1790–1860* (Cambridge, Mass.: MIT Press, 1982), XXVIII, XXIX.

© COPYRIGHT, The Center for Learning. Used with permission. Not for resale.

Document C

Imported goods were expensive. For everyday necessities the farmers continued to rely upon craftsmen in Rochester, and their insatiable demand turned the village into a manufacturing city. More than half the adult men in Rochester were skilled artisans, most of them engaged in turning local raw materials into finished goods for sale back to the countryside. The sixty-five workshops of 1823 concentrated on the necessities and little luxuries of rural life: guns and nails, shoes, hats, woolen cloth, wagons, furniture, farm tools—even jewelry and mirrors. These last testify to a growing prosperity and urbanity in the countryside. . . .

In 1820 most Rochesterians worked, played, and slept in the same place. There were no neighborhoods as we understand them: no distinct commercial and residential zones, no residential areas based upon social class. The integration of work and family life and of master and wage earner produced a nearly random mix of people and activities on the city's streets. . . .

The reorganization of work brought change into the most intimate corners of daily life. . . . On most jobs, employment was conditional on co-residence. Even workmen whose fathers and brothers headed households in Rochester lived with employers. Work, leisure, and domestic life were acted out in the same place and by the same people, and relations between masters and men transferred without a break from the workshop to the fireside. . . .

Wage earners were young and poor and numerous. Left alone, they might cause trouble. But with each of them a member of some household, and with householders answerable for the behavior of everyone under their care, the community could breathe easy. Public opinion held heads of families accountable for what their "children and dependents" did. . . .

Rochester proprietors had migrated from villages in which the public peace was secure. In the villages the more troublesome outsiders and dissidents were expelled. The others were governed by household heads, the disciplinary machinery of the church, and the web of community relationships. . .

Liquor was embedded in the pattern of irregular work and easy sociability sustained by the household economy. It was a bond between men who lived, worked, and played together, a compliment to the unique kind of domination associated with that round of life. Workmen drank with their employers, in situations that employers controlled. The informal mixing of work and leisure and of master and wage earner softened and helped legitimate inequality. At the same time drunkenness remained within the bounds of what the master considered appropriate. . . .

In the early years, disorder and insubordination were held in check, for master and wage earner worked together and slept under the same roof. Fights between workmen were rare, and when they occurred masters witnessed the intelligible and personal stream of events that led up to them. Wage earners loafed or drank or broke the Sabbath only with the master's knowledge and tacit consent. When workers lived with proprietors or within sight of them, serious breaches of the peace or of accepted standards of labor discipline were uncommon. At the very least, workingmen were constrained to act like guests, and masters enforced order easily, in the course of ordinary social and economic transactions. . . .

A generation of change . . . transformed Jefferson's republic of self-governing communities into Jackson's boisterous capitalist democracy. . . .

Established churches, stable neighborhoods, families, authoritative local elites: these and internalized restraints of every kind were swept away by the market, by migration and personal ambition, and by the universal acceptance of democratic ideas. . . .

Advanced Placement U.S. History 1 Name_____
Lesson 17 Date_____
Handout 17 (page 3)

> The drinking problem of the late 1820s stemmed directly from the new relationship between master and wage earner. Alcohol had been a builder of morale in household workshops, a subtle and pleasant bond between men. But in the 1820s proprietors turned their workshops into little factories, moved their families away from their places of business, and devised standards of discipline, self-control, and domesticity that banned liquor. By default, drinking became part of an autonomous working-class social life, and its meaning changed. . . .
>
> By 1830 the household economy had all but passed out of existence, and so had the social order that it sustained. Work, family life, the makeup of neighborhoods—the whole pattern of society—separated class from class: master and wage earner inhabited distinct social worlds. Workmen experienced new kinds of harassment on the job. But after work they entered a fraternal, neighborhood-based society in which they were free to do what they wanted. At the same time masters devised standards of work discipline, domestic privacy, and social peace that were directly antithetical to the spontaneous and noisy sociability of the workingmen. The two worlds stood within a few yards of each other, and they fought constantly.
>
> Paul E. Johnson, *A Shopkeeper's Millenium: Society and Revivals in Rochester, New York: 1815-1837* (New York: Hill and Wang, 1978), 9, 19, 48, 43, 44, 62, 55, 56-57, 60, 139.

1. Why did American observers find the early English factory system objectionable?

2. What specific factors suggested by the readings softened the social effects of the early Industrial Revolution in America?

3. What vision did early mill owners have about maintaining social control in the ideal industrial community?

© COPYRIGHT, The Center for Learning. Used with permission. Not for resale.

Advanced Placement U.S. History 1
Lesson 17
Handout 17 (page 4)

Name_____
Date_____

4. What safety valves provided an escape for discontented American workers and lessened exploitation of laborers in the United States in the early 1800s?

5. What caused the character of the Industrial Revolution in the United States to change from one of concern to one of exploitation?

6. Many persons, including Thomas Jefferson, feared the social effects of the Industrial Revolution on American civilization. What impact did Jefferson believe this economic change would have on the idyllic agrarian life style? (Use other references to answer this question.)

7. Were Jefferson and other critics of industrialization justified in their concerns about the impact of industrialization? Explain your answer.

Advanced Placement U.S. History 1
Lesson 18
Handout 18 (page 1)

Name_____
Date_____

The Evolution of Democracy from Jefferson to Jackson

Part A.

Complete the chart below to organize your research about the differences between Jeffersonian Democracy and Jacksonian Democracy.

Questions	Jeffersonian Democracy	Jacksonian Democracy
Political To what extent was universal white manhood suffrage achieved?		
Which citizens were considered eligible for office holding?		
How were candidates for president chosen?		
Economic In what way did Jackson expand the concept of the "chosen class"?		
How did each man view industrialization?		
How did the *Charles River Bridge v. Warren Bridge* decision affect the access to corporate charters prevalent in Jefferson's time?		
What was each man's attitude toward the Bank of the United States?		

© COPYRIGHT, The Center for Learning. Used with permission. Not for resale.

Advanced Placement U.S. History 1
Lesson 18
Handout 18 (page 2)

Name_____
Date_____

Questions	Jeffersonian Democracy	Jacksonian Democracy
Social What was each man's attitude toward slavery?		
What was each man's attitude toward equality for women and Native Americans?		
How did each man view education?		
How did each hope to remove obstacles to upward social mobility?		
Religious To what extent was separation of church and state accomplished in each period?		

Advanced Placement U.S. History 1
Lesson 18
Handout 18 (page 3)

Name_____
Date_____

Part B.

Use your completed chart from part A to help you answer the interpretive questions below.

1. In what respects was Jacksonian Democracy more democratic than Jeffersonian Democracy?

2. In what ways did each of the following contribute to the growth of democracy between 1800 and 1840?

    a. State constitutions

    b. *Charles River Bridge v. Warren Bridge* decision

    c. Changes in political party procedures

    d. Actions taken by Jackson himself

3. To what extent was Andrew Jackson responsible for changes in the period often called Jacksonian Democracy?

4. Did democratic changes in the "Age of Jackson" have greater political or economic impact? Explain your answer.

5. Both Jefferson and Jackson used the slogan "Equal rights for all, special privileges for none." In what respects did neither one achieve his goals?

6. How did the periods of Jeffersonian Democracy and Jacksonian Democracy illustrate the ideas that democracy is a process rather than a conclusion?

Advanced Placement U.S. History 1
Lesson 19
Handout 19 (page 1)

Name_____
Date_____

Purifying the Nation

Part A.

The list below contains names of reformers of the early nineteenth century. Select one person and, for homework, research answers to the following questions in preparation for a short classroom presentation.

Questions

1. What criticism of American society did the individual have?
2. What methods did the person use to improve American life?
3. What success did the individual have in promoting reform?
4. What detail(s) of the person's work made him or her an interesting historical figure?
5. To what extent was the reformer obsessed with achieving an impractical goal through fanatical or impractical means?
6. What lasting impact did the person's reforms have on American society?

Reformers

1. Lyman Beecher
2. Father Theobald Mathew
3. Neal Dow
4. Dorothea Dix
5. William Lloyd Garrison
6. Wendell Phillips
7. Theodore Weld
8. Sarah and Angelina Grimke
9. Frederick Douglass
10. Harriet Tubman
11. Harriet Beecher Stowe
12. Elijah Lovejoy
13. Elizabeth Cady Stanton
14. Lucretia Mott
15. Robert Owen
16. George Ripley
17. John Humphrey Noyes
18. Horace Mann
19. Elihu Burritt
20. Dr. Sylvester Graham

© COPYRIGHT, The Center for Learning. Used with permission. Not for resale.

Advanced Placement U.S. History 1 Name_____
Lesson 19 Date_____
Handout 19 (page 2)

Part B.

The following questions will help to put the reformers of the early nineteenth century in historical perspective.

1. List several evils that the reformers of the period 1820–1860 tried to eliminate.

2. What factors created a climate favorable to reform in the early nineteenth century?

3. What common vision of a better world did these individuals have?

4. Would you characterize these individuals as idealists or practical reformers? Explain your reasoning.

5. To what extent did these reformers achieve success in the period 1820–1860?

6. To what extent did these individuals build a foundation for the realization of reforms in a later period?

© COPYRIGHT, The Center for Learning. Used with permission. Not for resale.

Advanced Placement U.S. History 1
Lesson 20
Handout 20 (page 1)

Name_____
Date_____

The Mexican War—Was It in the National Interest?

Part A.

Use the following documents as a resource in completing the chart that follows on the arguments for and against American expansion to the Pacific, even at the expense of war with Mexico, in the 1840s.

Document A

But I am in danger of running into unnecessary details, which my debility will not enable me to close. The question is full of interest, also, as it affects our domestic relations and as it may bear upon those of Mexico to us. I will not undertake to follow it out to its consequences in those respects, though I must say that, in all aspects, the annexation of Texas to the United States promises to enlarge the circle of free institutions, and is essential to the United States, particularly as lessening the probabilities of future collision with foreign powers, and giving them greater efficiency in spreading the blessings of peace.

Andrew Jackson in a letter to Cong. Aaron V. Brown of Tennessee,
February 12, 1843

Document B

John L. O'Sullivan, the influential Democratic editor who gave the movement its name, wrote in 1845 that the American claim to new territory

. . . is by the right of our manifest destiny to overspread and to possess the whole of the continent which Providence has given us for the development of the great experiment of liberty and federative self government entrusted to us. It is a right such as that of the tree to the space of air and earth suitable for the full expansion of its principle and destiny of growth.

Richard N. Current et al., *A Survey of American History*, Vol. 1,
6th ed. (New York: Alfred A. Knopf, 1983), 375.

Document C

"We love to indulge in thoughts of the future extent and power of this Republic—because with its increase is the increase of human happiness and liberty. . . . What has miserable, inefficient Mexico—with her superstition, her burlesque upon freedom, her actual tyranny by the few over the many—what has she to do with the great mission of peopling the New World with a noble race? Be it ours, to achieve that mission! Be it ours to roll down all of the upstart leaven of old despotism, that comes our way!"

Walt Whitman, Editorial, *Brooklyn Daily Eagle*, July 7, 1846

© COPYRIGHT, The Center for Learning. Used with permission. Not for resale.

Document D

For American expansion to the Pacific was always a precise and calculated movement. It was ever limited in its objectives. American diplomatic and military policy that secured the acquisition of both Oregon and California was in the possession of men who never defined their expansionist purposes in terms of a democratic ideal. The vistas of all from Jackson to Polk were maritime and they were always anchored to specific waterways along the Pacific Coast. Land was necessary to them merely as a right of way to ocean ports—a barrier to be spanned by improved avenues of commerce. Any interpretation of westward extension beyond Texas is meaningless unless defined in terms of commerce and harbors.

> Norman A. Graebner, "The Land-Hunger Thesis Challenged," in *The Mexican War: Was It Manifest Destiny?* ed. by Ramon Eduardo Ruiz (New York: Holt, Reinhardt and Winston, 1963), 48.

Document E

However superior the Anglo-American race may be to that of Mexico, this gives the Americans no right to infringe upon the rights of the inferior race. The people of the United States may rightfully, and will, if they use the proper means, exercise a most beneficial moral influence over the Mexicans and other less enlightened nations of America. Beyond this they have no right to go.

> Albert Gallatin, "The Mission of the United States," in *Selected Readings in Great Issues in American History 1620–1968* from *Annals of America* (Chicago, Illinois: Encyclopaedia Britannica Educational Corporation, 1969), D-25.

Document F

"Then—Resolve,—Thet we wunt hev an inch o'slave territory;

Thet Presidunt Polk's holl perceedins air very tory;

Thet the war is a damned war, an' them thet enlist in it

Should hev a cravat with a dreffle tight twist in it;

Thet the war is a war fer the spreadin' o' slavery;"

> James Russell Lowell, *The Biglow Papers*, 1846

Document G

Less than a year before he became President, Lincoln wrote that "the act of sending an armed force among the Mexicans was unnecessary, inasmuch as Mexico was in no way molesting or menacing the United States or the people thereof; and that it was unconstitutional, because the power of levying war is vested in Congress, and not in the President" (June 1, 1860).

> Abraham Lincoln quoted in *The American Pageant* by Thomas A. Bailey and David M. Kennedy (Lexington, Massachusetts: D.C. Heath Company, 1983), 268.

Document H

Long-memoried Mexicans have never forgotten that their northern enemy tore away about half of their country. The argument that they were lucky not to lose all of it, and that they had been paid something for their land, did not lessen their bitterness. The war also marked an ugly turning point in the relations between the United States and Latin America as a whole. Hitherto, Uncle Sam had been regarded with some complacency, even friendliness. Henceforth, he was increasingly feared as the "Colossus of the North." Suspicious neighbors to the south condemned him as a greedy and untrustworthy bully, who might next despoil them of their soil.

> Bailey and Kennedy, *American Pageant*, 272.

© COPYRIGHT, The Center for Learning. Used with permission. Not for resale.

Advanced Placement U.S. History 1
Lesson 20
Handout 20 (page 3)

Name_____
Date_____

Document I

Within the United States, indecision about how much territory the country should demand also impeded rapid settlement. At the beginning of the war, ambitions of most Americans were relatively modest: California and New Mexico. But with each new, dazzling victory, the national appetite grew until "All Mexico" became a powerful slogan and movement.

The reluctance of most Americans to take on the responsibility of governing an alien, non-English-speaking people with different institutions and traditions, ultimately decided the All Mexico issue. Racism clearly played a part in the decision: Mexicans were "half-breeds," incapable of self-government; they would be a dead weight around the bounding young America's neck.

Irwin Unger, *These United States, Vol. 1*
(Boston, Massachusetts: Little, Brown and Company, 1973), 390–91.

Arguments for American expansion	Arguments against American expansion

Advanced Placement U.S. History 1
Lesson 20
Handout 20 (page 4)

Name_____
Date_____

Part B.

Based on your chart in part A, write a paragraph below on the following question: To what extent did the Mexican War promote the national interest?

Part C.

What values in the American character seemed to be portrayed by contemporary opinion-makers at the time of the Mexican War? List several values below.

Advanced Placement U.S. History 1
Lesson 20
Handout 20 (page 5)

Name_____
Date_____

Part D.

To conclude this lesson, examine your own paragraph in part B and answer the following questions:

a. What personal values are reflected in your paragraph on the extent to which the Mexican War promoted the national interest?

b. To what extent are your own values different from those of opinion-makers in the 1840s? Explain your view.

© COPYRIGHT, The Center for Learning. Used with permission. Not for resale.

Advanced Placement U.S. History 1
Lesson 21
Handout 21 (page 1)

Name_____
Date_____

Enlarging the National State

Part A.

Today, Americans unanimously accept the present territorial boundaries of the continental United States. That was not always the case. Opponents of expansion objected to the acquisition of each piece of land. However, the dominant theme in the country's past has always been expansion. Research each of the following acquisitions of the United States and complete the chart below to show how the United States accomplished this expansion to the Pacific.

Territory	Date acquired	Previous owner	Circumstances of acquisition
Original United States			
Louisiana Purchase			
British Cession			
Spanish Cession			
Texas Annexation			
Oregon Country			
Mexican Cession			
Gadsden Purchase			

Advanced Placement U.S. History 1
Lesson 21
Handout 21 (page 2)

Name_____
Date_____

Part B.

On the outline map that follows, locate, label, and outline (or color) each of the territorial acquisitions listed in the chart in part A.

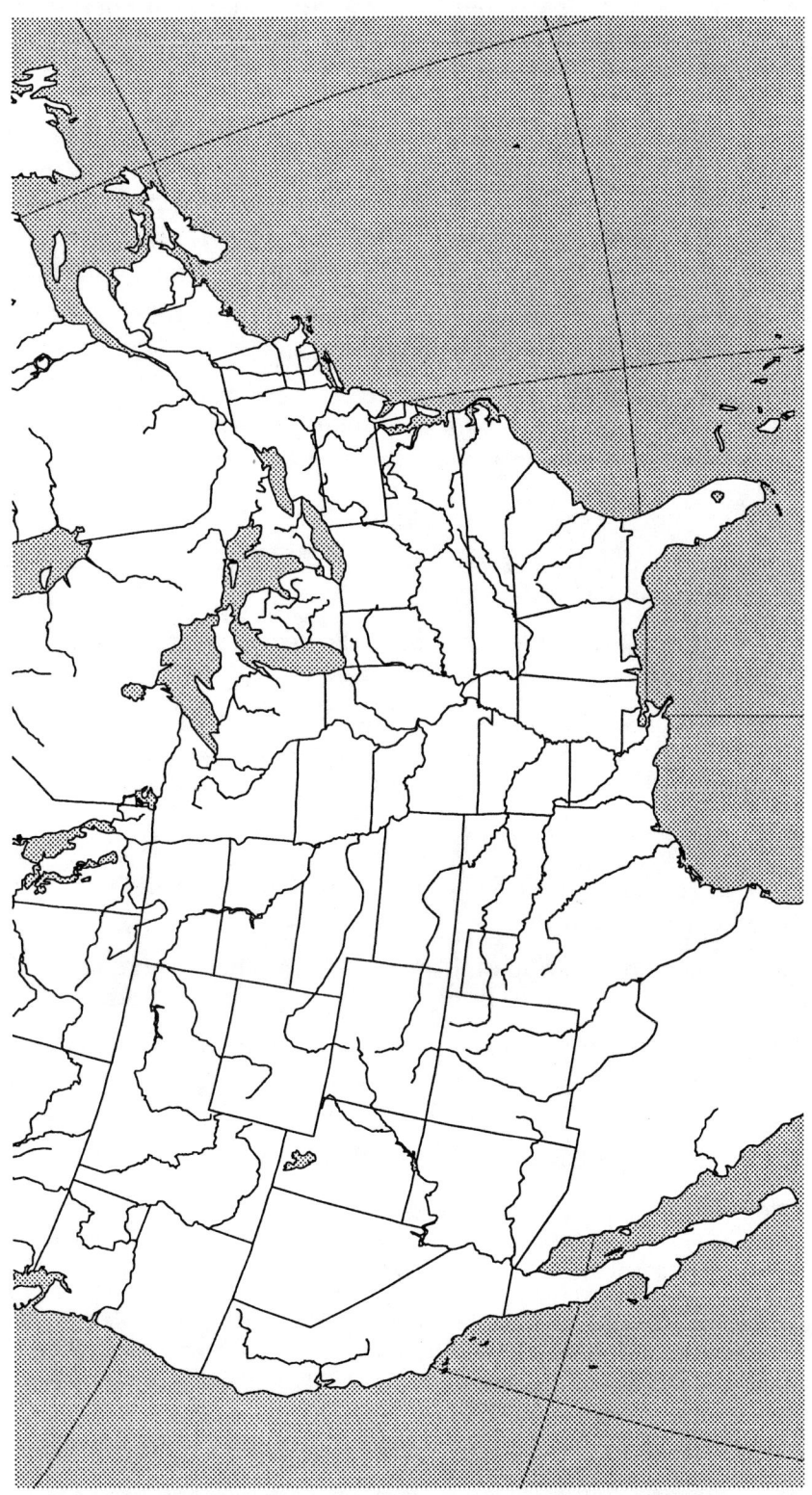

Advanced Placement U.S. History 1
Lesson 21
Handout 21 (page 3)

Name_____
Date_____

Part C.

Read the overview or sectional framework and then read the vignettes of three typical individuals. You will need to explain how each of three men, James Watson, Richard Fitzhugh, and George Hicks, would react to each of eight sectional issues of the ante-bellum period. Complete the chart by writing each man's position and rationale on each issue. You will use your completed chart to help you in answering the concluding questions in part D.

Sectional Framework for the Ante-bellum Period

East

Political—The region developed a broad-based democracy as property qualifications for voting were either reduced or eliminated for white males.

Economic—The area's diversified economy included commerce, banking, manufacturing, forest and mining products and stable, family-sized farms.

Social—A wide class structure ranged from wealthy businessmen to a few remaining indentured servants. Public schools, as well as a number of universities, had developed, and urban centers with a cultural and intellectual base were emerging.

South

Political—An aristocratic form of government, which had existed since colonial times, was well-established by the nineteenth century.

Economic—The planter aristocracy dominated the economy and produced a staple crop with slave labor. However, most whites lived a marginal existence on small farms.

Social—Few centers of learning or urban centers existed in this agrarian setting. A small percentage of white planters ran the establishment. Yeoman farmers yearned to become planters and supported slavery to keep African Americans in a subordinate position.

West

Political—A democratic society based on white male suffrage developed, but African Americans and women were not granted the right to vote.

Economic—Farms, owned and operated by the family, used large-scale agriculture and the new machinery of the period to produce food for eastern markets.

Social—While a few cities developed as centers of commerce, most people lived a rural life. The Northwest Ordinance had placed an emphasis on education. In the early 1830s, Oberlin College became the first college to admit women and African Americans.

These descriptions characterize the typical individuals shown on the chart:

James Watson

A manufacturer of cotton textiles in Pawtucket, Rhode Island, Watson is the son of an early factory owner who recognized the value of the cotton spinning machine for which Samuel Slater smuggled plans out of England. The elder Mr. Watson started a small mill in 1812 and, with the help of his son, James, expanded the mill threefold and began spinning, weaving and dying cloth. James Watson sees the possibility of further expansion as transportation makes markets more readily available.

© COPYRIGHT, The Center for Learning. Used with permission. Not for resale.

Advanced Placement U.S. History 1
Lesson 21
Handout 21 (page 4)

Name_____
Date_____

George Hicks

George Hicks recently moved to Indiana from Vermont where he had operated a small general farm. He purchased new farm machinery and two hundred acres on the Wabash River. With the help of his son, he grows wheat for sale in the East. He transports his produce via the Wabash and Erie Canal, the Great Lakes and the Erie Canal to eastern markets. With the influx of immigrants and the growth of cities in the East, Hicks is considering expanding his acreage in hopes of further increasing his profits.

Richard Fitzhugh

In 1849, Richard Fitzhugh inherited a plantation from his father. The nearly three thousand acres are situated on the banks of the Savannah River in Georgia. Fitzhugh has two hundred slaves, including 150 field hands. Mr. Fitzhugh is descended from an old line of southern plantation owners whose ancestors originally worked plantations in the tobacco lands of Virginia. He is a well-educated gentleman, having graduated from the College of William and Mary where he learned the values and practices of the southern code of chivalry.

Issue	Watson	Hicks	Fitzhugh
1. The national government should pass high tariffs.			
2. The national government should encourage settlement of small farms in the West.			
3. The national government should complete the nation's Manifest Destiny and prepare the new acquisitions for eventual statehood.			
4. The national government should promote internal improvements, including roads, canals, and railroads, at government expense.			

© COPYRIGHT, The Center for Learning. Used with permission. Not for resale.

Advanced Placement U.S. History 1
Lesson 21
Handout 21 (page 5)

Name_____
Date_____

Issue	Watson	Hicks	Fitzhugh
5. The national government should abolish slavery.			
6. The national government should promote technology.			
7. The national government should promote unlimited immigration to this country.			
8. The national government should promote universal education.			

© COPYRIGHT, The Center for Learning. Used with permission. Not for resale.

Advanced Placement U.S. History 1 Name_____
Lesson 21 Date_____
Handout 21 (page 6)

Part D.

To conclude this lesson, use your completed chart to answer the following questions:

1. How did the definition of "West" change in the years 1800 to 1860?

2. What were the assets of continental expansion?

3. What negatives accompanied new territorial acquisitions?

4. How did Henry Clay's American System help to promote national unity?

5. How did the social structure change more dramatically in the North than in the South in the decades before the Civil War?

6. How would you characterize the emerging position of the West within the Union during the decades before the Civil War?

7. How did the increasing regionalization of the nation create difficulties for the national government?

Advanced Placement U.S. History 1
Lesson 22
Handout 22 (page 1)

Name_____
Date_____

Compromise and Conflict—The Road to War

An eighth-grade history teacher has appealed to your teacher for help. This eighth-grade teacher would like your class to prepare an illustrated presentation for eighth-grade students on causes of the Civil War. You could do much to motivate these students by serving as role models of creativity and scholarship. Your teacher, knowing that the best way to learn a subject is to teach it, was happy to cooperate.

Dividing yourselves into four groups will be useful. However, before you work in groups, the class as a whole needs to do some initial planning.

1. Begin by deciding how you will complete The Road to War sheet at the end of this handout. Copies of this sheet will be distributed to the students you teach.

   a. You will need to decide what issue led to each of the following:

      Compromise of 1820

      Compromise of 1833

      Compromise of 1850

   b. What map or other symbols might represent each of the above issues to make the diagram easier for eighth graders to follow?

   c. What were the terms of each of the above compromises?

   d. What are the eight or ten most significant events of the 1850s that your class will stress in explaining how an irreconcilable conflict led to war between the North and South in 1861?

2. Now divide into four groups.

   Group A
   The task of this group is to prepare one transparency to clarify each of the points on The Road to War. These might be drawings, before and after maps, cartoons, or other visuals. In the presentation this group is responsible for presenting the "facts" of the controversies and compromises.

   Group B
   The task of this group is to write a script and prepare one member of the group to present the Northern reasoning in a mini-debate on each of the issues on The Road to War. You might choose, for example, to role-play a particular Northerner editor. Try to be as creative as possible and still retain authenticity. Remember your audience!

   Group C
   This group has the task of writing a script and preparing one member of the group to present the Southern reasoning in a mini-debate on each of the issues on The Road to War. You may choose, for example, to represent a particular individual or a typical planter of the times. You, too, want to strive for authenticity and creativity to convey your point to your young audience.

   Group D
   The task of this group is to act as present-day historians well-versed on causes of the Civil War. In addition to conducting the class session in an orderly manner with appropriate time allotments for each group, this group, or one member, also makes a final interpretive assessment of the most important reasons for the outbreak of war, presents possible ways war might have been avoided, explains how delays resulting from the compromises likely affected the outcome of the war, and why the war may have been the most significant chapter in our nation's history. Your group needs to plan how to handle questions at the end of your class.

© COPYRIGHT, The Center for Learning. Used with permission. Not for resale.

Advanced Placement U.S. History 1
Lesson 22
Handout 22 (page 2)

Name_____
Date_____

The Road to War

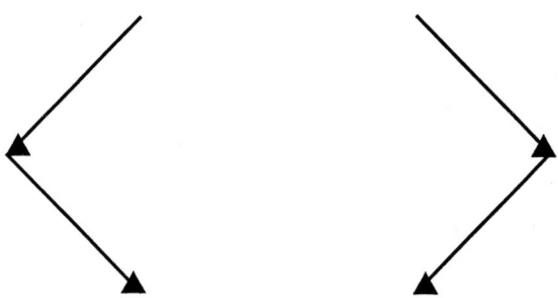

Compromise of 1820

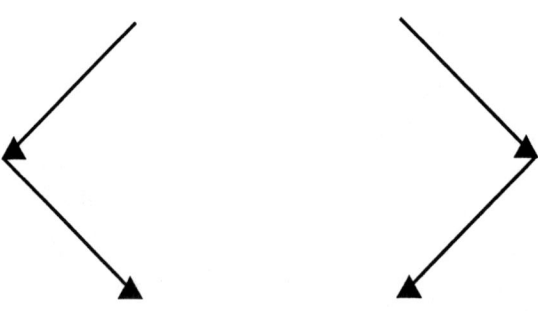

Compromise of 1833

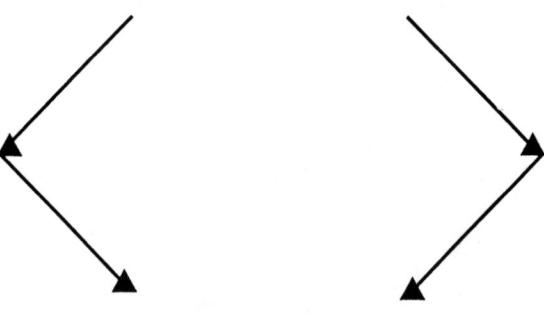

Compromise of 1850

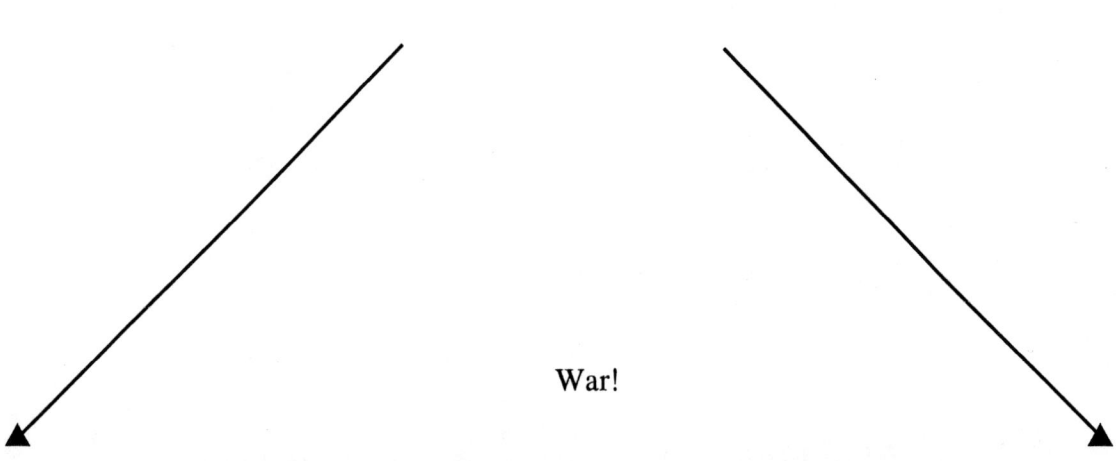

War!

Advanced Placement U.S. History 1
Lesson 23
Handout 23 (page 1)

Name_____
Date_____

Abolition—The Role of the Individual in Effecting Change

Part A.

Review your notes on the abolitionists in Lesson 19 to answer the following questions.

1. Explain both a moral and a political rationale for abolition.

    a. Moral

    b. Political

2. Explain why several of these abolitionists were involved in more than one reform movement.

3. List five or six methods, strategies, or tactics the abolitionists used to sway public opinion in support of their cause.

Part B.

Read the following documents as a resource in answering the questions at the end.

Document A

That the normal condition of all the territory of the United States is that of freedom: That, as our Republican fathers, when they had abolished slavery in all our national territory, ordained that "no persons should be deprived of life, liberty or property without due process of law," it becomes our duty, by legislation, whenever such legislation is necessary, to maintain this provision of the Constitution against all attempts to violate it; and we deny the authority of Congress, of a territorial legislature, or of any individuals, to give legal existence to slavery in any territory of the United States.

Republican Party Platform, 1860

Document B

Apprehension seems to exist among the people of the Southern states, that by the accession of a Republican Administration their property, and their peace, and personal security, are to be endangered. There has never been any reasonable cause for such apprehension. Indeed, the most ample evidence to the contrary has all the while existed . . . in nearly all the published speeches of him who now addresses you. I do but quote from one of those speeches when I declare that "I have no purpose, directly or indirectly, to interfere with the institution of slavery in the states where it exists. I believe I have no lawful right to do so, and I have no inclination to do so."

The proposition that . . . the Union is perpetual, [is] confirmed by the history of the Union itself. The Union is much older than the Constitution. It was formed in fact, by the Articles of Association in 1774. It was matured and continued by the Declaration of Independence in 1776. It was further matured and the faith of all the then thirteen states expressly plighted and engaged that it should be perpetual, by the Articles of Confederation in 1778. And finally, in 1787, one of the declared objects for ordaining and establishing the Constitution, was "to form a more perfect Union."

It follows from these views that no state, upon its own mere motion, can lawfully get out of the Union; that resolves and ordinances to that effect are legally void, and that acts of violence, within any state or states, against the authority of the United States, are insurrectionary [rebellious] or revolutionary, according to circumstances.

I therefore consider that in view of the Constitution and the laws, the Union is unbroken; and to the extent of my ability I shall take care, as the Constitution itself expressly enjoins upon [directs] me, that the laws of the Union be faithfully executed in all the states.

Lincoln's First Inaugural, March 4, 1861

Document C

When Lincoln last determined, in July 1862, to move toward emancipation, it was only after all his other policies had failed. The Crittenden Resolution had been rejected, the border states had quashed his plan of compensated emancipation, his generals were still floundering, and he had already lost the support of great numbers of conservatives. The Proclamation became necessary to hold his remaining supporters and to forestall—so he believed—English recognition of the Confederacy. "I would save the Union," he wrote in answer to Horace Greeley's cry for emancipation. ". . . If I could save the Union without freeing any slaves, I would do it; and if I could save it by freeing all the slaves, I would do it." In the end, freeing all the slaves seemed necessary.

Richard Hofstadter, American Political Tradition
(New York: Alfred Knopf, 1948), 130.

Document D

"That on the first day of January, in the year of our Lord one thousand eight hundred and sixty-three, all persons held as slaves within any State, or designated part of a State, the people whereof shall then be in rebellion against the United States, shall be then, thenceforward, and forever, free; and the Executive Government of the United States, including the military and naval authority thereof, will recognize and maintain the freedom of such persons, and will do no act or acts to repress such persons, or any of them, in any efforts they may make for their actual freedom."

Emancipation Proclamation, January 1, 1863

Document E

For all its limitations, the Emancipation Proclamation probably made genuine emancipation inevitable. In all but five of the states freedom was accomplished in fact through the Thirteenth Amendment. Lincoln's own part in the passing of this amendment was critical. He used all his influence to get the measure the necessary two-thirds vote in the House of Representatives, and it was finally carried by a margin of three votes. Without his influence the amendment might have been long delayed, though it is hardly conceivable that it could have been held off indefinitely.

Hofstadter, American Political Tradition, 132.

Advanced Placement U.S. History 1
Lesson 23
Handout 23 (page 3)

Name_____
Date_____

1. Explain Lincoln's position on slavery in the 1860 Republican platform.

2. According to his First Inaugural in 1861, what was Lincoln's primary objective when he took office?

3. When Lincoln issued the Emancipation Proclamation, what was his motive?

4. To which states did the Emancipation apply?

5. Why did the Emancipation Proclamation not free any slaves immediately?

6. What role did Lincoln play in enacting the Thirteenth Amendment?

7. Lincoln has often been referred to as the "Great Emancipator." Which of his actions primarily accounts for his holding that title? Explain your answer.

Part C.

After reviewing your answers in parts A and B, develop a one-paragraph thesis on the role of individuals in accomplishing the abolition of slavery.

© COPYRIGHT, The Center for Learning. Used with permission. Not for resale.

Advanced Placement U.S. History 1
Lesson 24
Handout 24 (page 1)

Name_____
Date_____

The "Failure" of Radical Reconstruction

Part A.

Your group's task is to prepare a presentation supporting the argument of Eric McKitrick. Try to lead your audience to a logical conclusion regarding the "failure" of Radical Reconstruction and its implications for the nation's future. Buttress your argument with at least five telling pieces of evidence. Appropriate supportive data might take the form of particularly moving pictures, short readings, cartoons, public documents, charts, graphs, or diary entries. Guidelines are offered to help you organize your presentation.

Eric McKitrick contends that Radical Reconstruction, which was designed to bring about a social revolution in race relations, failed to help the African American find his or her proper place in American life. He cites three reasons for this failure: confused priorities, opposition from southern whites, and the federal government's unwillingness to maintain the long-term pressure necessary to accomplish Radical Republican goals.

1. Begin by acknowledging real accomplishments of Radical Republicans during the years 1865–1877.

2. Contrast Radical Republican goals with steps that might better have prepared African Americans for successful integration into American society politically, economically, and socially.

3. Demonstrate the extent to which southern whites were forced to accept, for a time, regimes they did not want.

4. Explain why commitment to Radical Republican Reconstruction ended and why Reconstruction ended officially in 1877.

5. Conclude with your assessment of the implications of the end of Radical Reconstruction for African Americans in the South at that time and the implications for the future. Does your research help you to identify a major reason for the failure to accomplish the successful integration of African Americans into American life in the years immediately after the war?

© COPYRIGHT, The Center for Learning. Used with permission. Not for resale.

Advanced Placement U.S. History 1
Lesson 24
Handout 24 (page 2)

Name_____
Date_____

Part B.

In contrast to earlier historians who viewed Reconstruction in negative terms and focused on the era's tragedies and graft, corruption, high taxes, and huge public debts, revisionist historians have found much to admire in the preparations begun in the early postwar years to integrate African Americans into American society. Your group's task is to prepare a presentation analyzing the achievements of "Black Reconstruction." Buttress your argument with at least five telling pieces of evidence. Appropriate supportive data might take the form of particularly moving pictures, short readings, cartoons, public documents, charts, graphs, or diary entries. Guidelines are offered to help you organize your presentation.

1. Begin by defining the term "Black Reconstruction."

2. Analyze to what extent African American goals of education, economic development, and establishing and reaffirming community were achieved in the period 1865–1877.

3. Give examples that demonstrate the desire of African Americans to establish independence and gain control over their own lives and destinies.

4. In what ways did "Black Reconstruction" pave the way for the Civil Rights Movement of the 1960s?

5. How do you account for the fact that the achievements of "Black Reconstruction" were given so little recognition until recently?

Part 4
Developing the American Nation-State

With the nation-state politically secure, the nation focused on industrialization and the development of an interdependent national market. Using the philosophy of Social Darwinism, industrialists justified their creation of monopolies and exploitation of labor and resources. Big business control of government, combined with their monopolistic practices, resulted in rising protests from farmers, laborers, and radical critics of laissez-faire capitalism. Workers and farmers sought improvement in their conditions through organizations and political action, but African Americans and immigrants had few opportunities for improving their lot. Problems that developed during the Gilded Age set the agenda for change in the Progressive Movement of the early twentieth century.

By the conclusion of this unit, you should be able to answer the following basic questions:

- What accounts for America's transition to industrialism in the late nineteenth century?

- How did businessmen try to stabilize the growing chaos in the American economy in the late 1800s?

- How did big business control the national government at the expense of the masses during the Gilded Age?

- How did big businesses justify monopolies and exploitation of society?

- How did extreme actions of industrialists produce extreme proposals for reform?

- Why did early labor unions fail to gain wide acceptance?

- To what extent were the problems of farmers during the Gilded Age attributable to big business?

- To what extent did the Populists predict the future?

- Booker T. Washington's programs created more realistic opportunities for reform than did those of W.E.B. DuBois. Assess the validity of this position.

- How did the decorative and fine arts of the Gilded Age reflect the values of the era?

Advanced Placement U.S. History 1
Lesson 25
Handout 25 (page 1)

Name_____
Date_____

The Emergence of Industrial America

Listed below are a series of factors responsible for American industrialism in the late nineteenth century. First, explain the significance of each term. Then, examine the list, divide the items into three or four categories, and label the categories. Finally, write a thesis statement to account for the United States becoming the foremost industrial power in the world by 1900.

Factors Supporting Industrialism

a. Western mining

b. Immigration

c. Government subsidies and tax concessions to railroads

d. Advances in communication

e. Corporation charters

f. Laissez faire attitude of government

g. Bessemer process

h. New sources of power

i. High tariffs

j. Yankee ingenuity

k. Entrepreneurs

l. Vertical and horizontal integration

m. National markets

n. Civil War profits and foreign investment

Advanced Placement U.S. History 1
Lesson 25
Handout 25 (page 2)

Name_____
Date_____

Categories

Write here your thesis statement to account for the emergence of industrialism in America. Be sure to state what you believe to be the most important factor and state or imply its relationship to the other categories you developed in the above chart.

Advanced Placement U.S. History 1
Lesson 26
Handout 26 (page 1)

Name_____
Date_____

The Growing Economic Crisis of the Late Nineteenth Century

At the beginning of the twentieth century, financier J.P. Morgan sought a way to bring order and stability to what he considered the chaotic condition of American business. He summarized three major problems of American businessmen: (1) business had to be saved from ruinous competition; (2) the rise and fall of prices had to be minimized and the disastrous effects of the business cycle padded and (3) the rising power of labor had to be blocked at all costs, or capitalism would eventually give way to socialism. Morgan sought to organize holding companies in nearly every major industry as a way of helping entrepreneurs make savings in buying and manufacturing, control prices, and raise profits.

Study the documents in each section for information to answer the related questions at the end.

Part A.

Document A

The story of the early history of the oil trade is too well known to bear repeating in detail. The cleansing of crude petroleum was a simple and easy process, and at first the profits were very large. Naturally, all sorts of people went into it; the butcher, the baker, and the candlestick maker began to refine oil and it was only a short time before more of the finished product was put on the market than could possibly be consumed. The price went down and down until the trade was threatened with ruin. . . .

. . . this great depression led to consultations with our neighbors and friends in the business in the effort to bring some order out of what was rapidly becoming a state of chaos . . . we proceeded to buy the largest and best refining concerns and centralize the administration of them with a view to securing greater economy and efficiency. . . .

This enterprise, conducted by men of application and ability working hard together, soon built up unusual facilities in manufacture, in transportation, in finance, and in extending markets. . . .

John D. Rockefeller, *Random Reminiscences of Men and Events.*
(New York: Doubleday, 1909), 81–83.

Document B

The first and least formal method attempted was the *agreement*. By this each competitor agreed to certain standardized prices and policies; usually they were promptly broken when someone saw a chance to undersell his rivals. The next step, the pool, was a division of marketing areas, freight, or earnings; it also fell through when one member saw a chance to grab off a large order or to pre-empt a certain field, but it by no means was discarded and, indeed, the modern trade associations bear some resemblance to it.

The search for uniformity was next sought . . . by interlocking directorates. That is, the directors of any corporation sat upon the boards of allied corporations and strove to reconcile policies and minimize competitive clashes. The method was more successful than the others (and is still used), but it was cumbersome.

Leland D. Baldwin, *The Stream of American History, Vol. II*
(New York: American Book Company, 1952), 110.

Advanced Placement U.S. History 1
Lesson 26
Handout 26 (page 2)

Name_____
Date_____

Document C

It is too late to argue about advantages of industrial combinations. They are a necessity. . . . Their chief advantages are:

(1) Command of necessary capital.

(2) Extension of limits of business.

(3) Increase of number of persons interested in the business.

(4) Economy in the business.

(5) Improvements and economies which are derived from knowledge of many interested persons of wide experience.

(6) Power to give the public improved products at less prices and still make profit for stockholders.

(7) Permanent work and good wages for laborers.

> John D. Rockefeller's testimony, United States Industrial Commission, *Preliminary Reports on Trusts and Industrial Combinations.* House Document No. 476, 56th Congress, 1st Session (December, 1899), Part I, 796.

1. What did John D. Rockefeller believe was the key to stabilizing the oil industry?

2. What were the weaknesses of each of the following methods of stabilizing industry?

   a. agreement

   b. pool

   c. interlocking directorate

3. Why did Rockefeller perceive a trust to be a solution to the weaknesses of less formal attempts at business organization?

Advanced Placement U.S. History 1
Lesson 26
Handout 26 (page 3)

Name_____
Date_____

Part B.

Document D

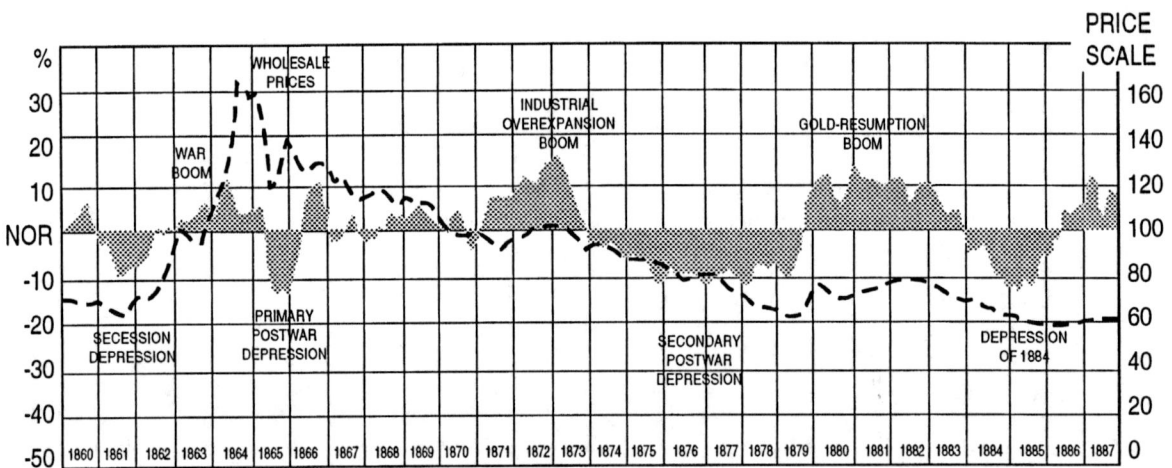

Baldwin, *Stream of American History*, Vol. II, 114.

Document E
Average Daily Earnings of Nonfarm Employees: 1870–1880

Year	Earnings
1870	$1.47
1871	1.45
1873	1.40
1876	1.21
1879	1.12
1880	1.16

Ben J. Wattenberg, ed. *The Statistical History of the United States from Colonial Times to the Present*, Vol. 1 (New York: Basic Books, 1976), 165.

Document F
Wholesale Prices of Selected Commodities, 1871–1879

Year	Coal (anthracite)	Steel Rails	Copper
1871	$4.46	$102.52	$.241
1872	3.74	111.94	.356
1876	3.87	59.25	.210
1879	2.70	48.21	.186

Wattenberg, *Statistical History*, 208.

© COPYRIGHT, The Center for Learning. Used with permission. Not for resale.

Advanced Placement U.S. History 1
Lesson 26
Handout 26 (page 4)

4. Explain why economists use the phrase "business cycle" to describe the economic activity shown in Document D.

5. Explain how daily wages in 1873 and 1879 relate to points on the graph of the business cycle.

6. Explain how prices of coal, steel rails, and copper in 1871, 1876, and 1879 relate to points on the graph of the business cycle.

7. From the documents, what inferences can you make about the "disastrous effects of the business cycle" for each group below:

   a. corporations

   b. workers

Advanced Placement U.S. History 1
Lesson 26
Handout 26 (page 5)

Name_____
Date_____

Part C.

Document G

Union Membership, 1870–1930			
Year	Average annual union membership	Number of workers, ten years and over, excluding agricultural workers	Union membership as a percentage of the total number of workers outside agriculture
1870	300,000*	6,075,000	4.9%
1880	200,000*	8,807,000	2.3%
1890	372,000*	13,380,000	2.7%
1900	868,000	18,161,000	4.8%
1910	2,140,000	25,779,000	8.3%
1920	5,048,000	30,985,000	16.3%
1930	3,393,000	38,358,000	8.8%

*Figures for 1870, 1880, and 1890 are estimates.

U.S. Bureau of the Census, *Historical Statistics of the United States, Colonial Times to 1957.* (Washington, DC: Government Printing Office, 1960), 72, 98.

Document H

. . . a system (should be) adopted which will secure to the laborer the fruits of his toil; and as this much-desired object can only be accomplished by the thorough unification of labor, and the united efforts of those who obey the divine injunction that "In the sweat of thy brow shalt thou eat bread," we have formed the Knights of Labor with a view of securing the organization and direction, by cooperative effort, of the power of the industrial classes; and we submit to the world the objects sought to be accomplished by our organization, calling upon all who believe in securing "the greatest good to the greatest number" to aid and assist us:—

I. To bring within the folds of organization every department of productive industry, making knowledge a stand-point for action, and industrial and moral worth, not wealth, the true standard of individual and national greatness.

II. To secure to the toilers a proper share of the wealth that they create; more of the leisure that rightfully belongs to them; more societary advantages; more of the benefits, privileges, and emoluments of the world; in a word, all those rights and privileges necessary to make them capable of enjoying, appreciating, defending and perpetuating the blessings of good government. . . .

IV. The establishment of cooperative institutions, productive and distributive.

Terence Powderly, president of the Knights of Labor
Richard N. Current, et al., *Words That Made American History,*
Vol. 2, 3rd ed. (Boston: Little, Brown, 1962), 102.

8. In what way do the above documents on labor union membership and the Knights of Labor philosophy reflect concerns of J.P. Morgan?

Part D.

Document I

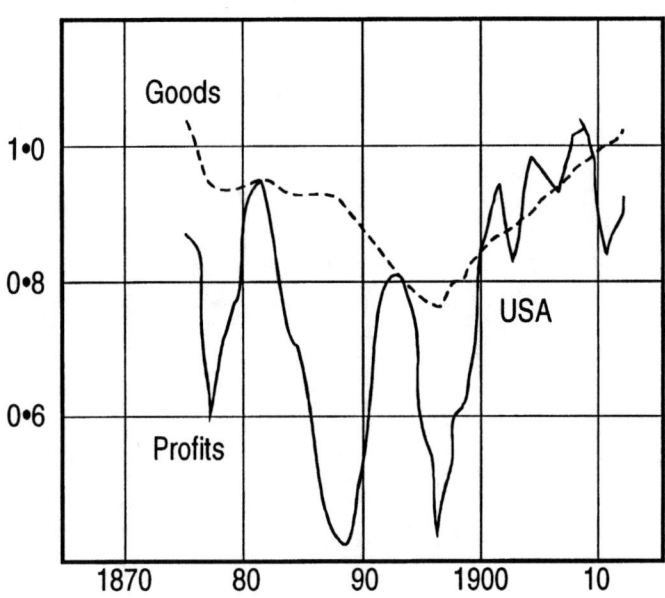

Profitability and Capital Goods

W. Arthur Lewis, *Growth and Fluctuations, 1870–1913*
(London: George Allen & Unwin, 1978), 102.

Document J

More likely than not, the average railroad president in the 1870s had a background in politics—over half held some political job before or during their careers as railroad presidents. Surely the ogre of government intervention could not have appeared too formidable to men with important political connections themselves and familiar with the intricacies and possibilities of politics.

Gabriel Kolko, *Railroads and Regulation, 1877–1916*
(Westport, CT: Greenwood Press, 1976), 15

Advanced Placement U.S. History 1
Lesson 26
Handout 26 (page 7)

Document K

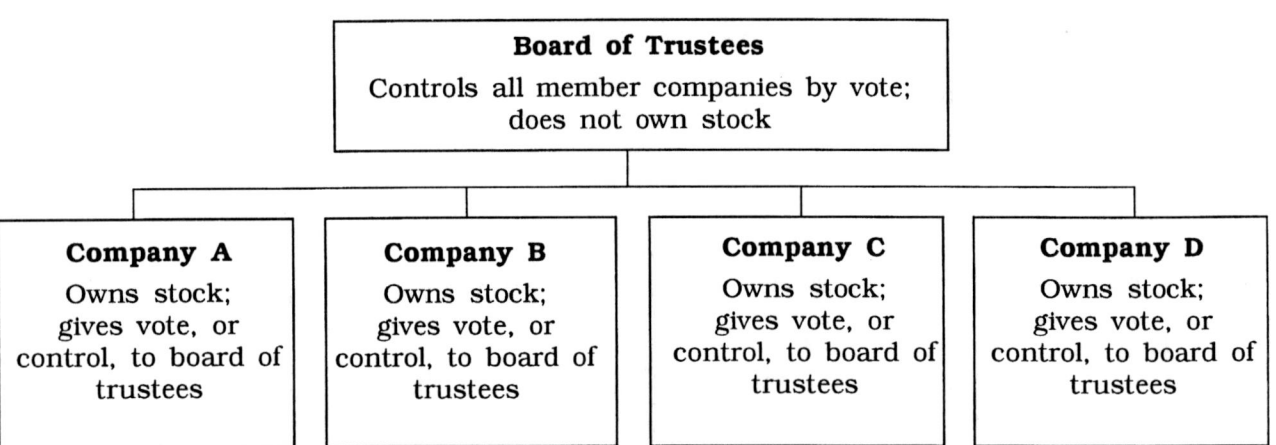

David C. King, et al., *United States History from 1865*
(Reading, Mass.: Addison-Wesley, 1986), 107.

Document L

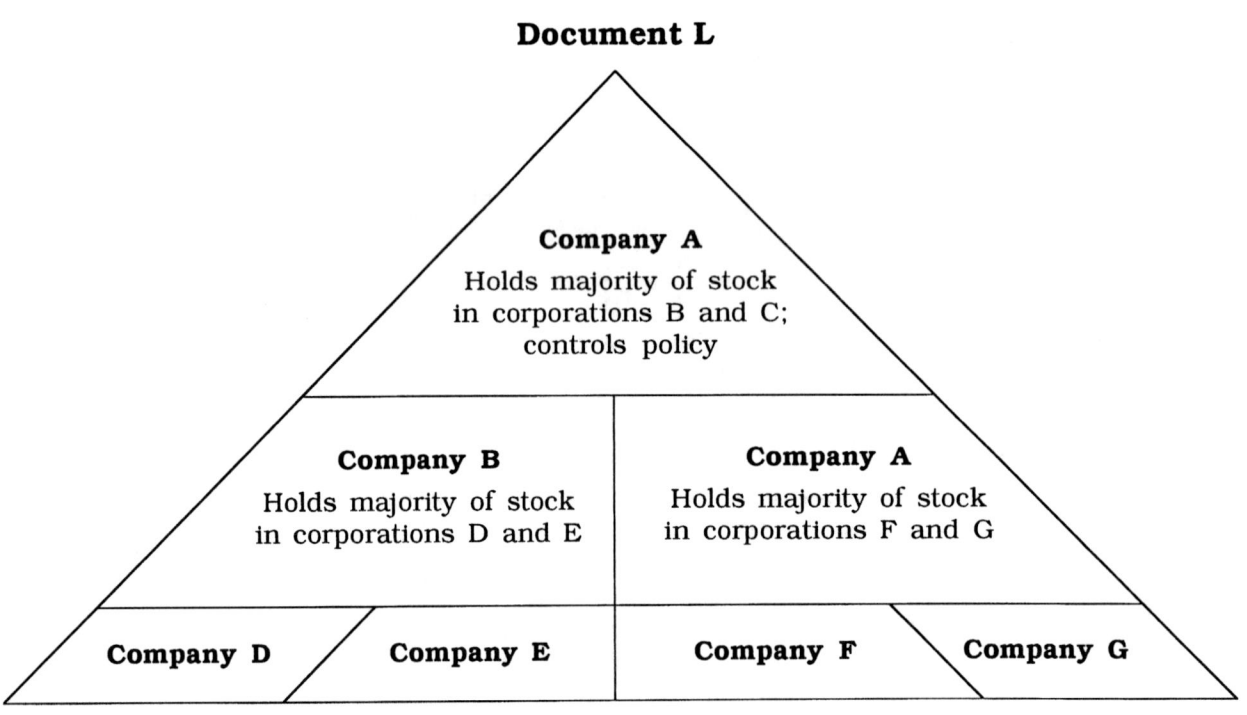

King, *United States History*, 110.

Advanced Placement U.S. History 1
Lesson 26
Handout 26 (page 8)

Name_____
Date_____

9. Even though Congress passed antitrust legislation, why did corporate leaders try to retain the concept of the trust?

10. How did corporate leaders hope to maintain the essence of trusts?

11. How does the relationship of a Board of Trustees to a trust (document K) differ from the relationship of a Board of Directors to a holding company (document L)?

12. Research why the Fourteenth Amendment was used to protect a holding company but not a trust.

Part E.

13. In what respect has the government adopted a broader perspective of economic problems than did J.P. Morgan?

14. How much economic freedom should society give to an individual to seek his or her own ends to the detriment of others?

15. In what respect do the actions of the government in the twentieth century reflect the failure of J.P. Morgan's philosophy of holding companies?

16. To conclude this lesson, write a thesis statement that explains why Morgan's approach to organizing the economy has not been accepted in the twentieth century.

Advanced Placement U.S. History 1
Lesson 27
Handout 27 (page 1)

Name_____
Date_____

National Government in the Late Nineteenth Century—
A Sham of Democracy

Part A.

Study the cartoon below and answer the questions at the end.

Daniel J. Boorstin and Brooks M. Kelley, *A History of the United States*
(Lexington, Mass.: Ginn and Company, 1986), 393.

1. Why are the trusts portrayed as vultures?

2. Why did the cartoonist use "$" instead of "S" in the word "Senate"?

3. How could the trusts purchase a Senate seat?

4. What bias did the Founding Fathers demonstrate in their procedure for electing senators?

5. How does the cartoon demonstrate the survival of the Founding Fathers' bias?

6. Explain how the cartoon reflects the cartoonist's biases.

© COPYRIGHT, The Center for Learning. Used with permission. Not for resale.

Part B.

Consider documents A and B and answer the question at the end.

Document A
Major Legislation and Court Decisions, 1862–1897

- The Morrill Tariff of 1861 raised duties to their 1846 levels; the McKinley Tariff of 1890 aimed to make duties so high that imports would be eliminated; the Dingley Tariff of 1897 raised rates to their highest level to date.

- The Bland-Allison Act of 1878, initially proposed in the House of Representatives to create an inflationary currency through unlimited coinage of silver, was amended by anti-inflationary forces in the Senate to restrict substantially the coinage of silver that farmers and miners wanted.

- The Interstate Commerce Act of 1887 forbade rebates, pools, long- and short-haul abuses, and discriminatory freight rates and created a commission to carry infractions of the law to the courts.

- The Sherman Antitrust Act of 1890 declared illegal every contract, combination in the form of trusts or otherwise, or conspiracy in restraint of trade or commerce.

- In *U.S. v. E.C. Knight* (1895), the Supreme Court ruled that manufacturing is not a conspiracy in restraint of trade and is, therefore, not covered under the Sherman Antitrust Act.

- In the *Maximum Freight Rate Case* (1897), the Supreme Court sheared the Interstate Commerce Commission of its presumed power to modify rates and forbade it to seek judicial aid in such cases.

Document B

Federal Prosecutions Instituted under the Sherman Antitrust Act, 1890–1901		
Presidential Administration	**Months in Office**	**Number of Cases**
Benjamin Harrison	32	7
Grover Cleveland	48	8
William McKinley	54	3

Hans B. Thorelli, *Federal Antitrust Policy: The Origination of an American Tradition* (1955).

What conclusion can you draw from the chart about the sympathies of the national government in the late nineteenth century?

Advanced Placement U.S. History 1
Lesson 27
Handout 27 (page 3)

Name_____
Date_____

Part C.

How would each of the following present-day democratic features have increased the influence of the masses in government in the late nineteenth century?

1. secret ballot

2. direct election of Senators

3. universal suffrage

4. direct primaries

5. initiative, referendum, and recall

Part D.

1. Draw a conclusion about the relationship of government to big business and to the masses in the late nineteenth century.

2. To conclude the lesson, create a cartoon or other visual to demonstrate this relationship among government, big business, and the masses and its implications for democracy in the late nineteenth century.

Advanced Placement U.S. History 1
Lesson 28
Handout 28 (page 1)

Name_____
Date_____

The Philosophy of the Industrialists

Part A.

Study the following readings and cartoons as a resource in answering the questions that follow.

Document A

(Adam) Smith was among the first to make a clear and convincing case that when individuals follow their own self-interest, it automatically works to the benefit of society as a whole. As individual competitors pursue their own maximum profit, they are all thus forced to be more efficient. This results in cheaper goods in the long run. Free competition in all markets and with all goods and services is thus to be encouraged; government intervention serves only to make operations less efficient and is thus to be avoided. The same principles apply to international trade. There should be a minimum of government interference in the way of duties, quotas, and tariffs. Smith's is the classical argument in support of free trade.

> Gerald F. Cavanagh, *American Business Values in Transition*
> (Englewood Cliffs, N.J.: Prentice-Hall, 1976), 42–43.

Document B

Herbert Spencer (1820–1903) proposed a harsh "survival of the fittest" philosophy. The bright and able contribute most to society, and so are to be encouraged and rewarded. The poor, the weak, and the handicapped demand more than they contribute, and so should not be supported but rather allowed to die a natural death. Contact with harsh and demanding reality is a maturing experience that should not be diluted by well-intentioned but in reality destructive charities and handouts. If "natural" principles were followed, evolution and the survival of the fittest in the competition of human life would be the result. Spencer did not set out to examine any particular society and its values; rather, his critique was proposed as "culture-free." According to Spencer, it applied to all people for it was derived from basic, organic principles of growth and development. Spencer applied to society the same principles that Charles Darwin saw in biological life—hence the name, Social Darwinism.

> Cavanagh, *American Business Values in Transition*, 11.

Document C

This, then, is held to be the duty of the man of Wealth: First, to set an example of modest, unostentatious living, shunning display or extravagance; to provide moderately for the legitimate wants of those dependent upon him; and after doing so to consider all surplus revenues which come to him simply as trust funds, which he is called upon to administer, and strictly bound as a matter of duty to administer in the manner which, in his judgment, is best calculated to produce the most beneficial results for the community—the man of wealth thus becoming the mere agent and trustee for his poorer brethren, bringing to their service his superior wisdom, experience, and ability to administer, doing for them better than they would or could do for themselves. . . .

> Andrew Carnegie, "Wealth," *North American Review*,
> CXLVIII (June, 1889), 661–662.

© COPYRIGHT, The Center for Learning. Used with permission. Not for resale.

Document D

Document E

"The growth of a large business is merely survival of the fittest. . . . The American Beauty Rose can be produced in the splendor and fragrance which bring cheer to its beholder only by sacrificing the early buds which grow up around it. This is not an evil tendency in business. It is merely the working-out of a law of nature and a law of God."

John D. Rockefeller's statement to his Sunday School class quoted in William H. Ghent, *Our Benevolent Feudalism* (New York: Macmillan, 1903), 29.

Document F

Advanced Placement U.S. History 1
Lesson 28
Handout 28 (page 3)

Name_____
Date_____

Document G

The Gospel of Wealth. Cartoon from *Judge*, 1903. Andrew Carnegie in Scottish attire shovels out 100 million dollars for libraries and other good works.
(Courtesy of the New York Public Library.)

1. Summarize in a sentence or two the philosophy of each of the following:

   a. Laissez-faire capitalism

   b. Social Darwinism

   c. Gospel of Wealth

2. How does Social Darwinism reinforce laissez-faire?

3. How does the Gospel of Wealth help to justify the philosophy of Social Darwinism?

Advanced Placement U.S. History 1
Lesson 28
Handout 28 (page 4)

4. Based on research about John D. Rockefeller, state several specific business practices that Rockefeller seems to justify in his comment to his Sunday School class.

5. How did the cartoonist interpret John D. Rockefeller's remark?

6. Answer the following questions about the cartoon on King Monopoly:

   a. What does the cartoonist imply was the source of the monopolist's wealth and power?

   b. What industries does the cartoonist show as protected businesses?

   c. What does the booty in the cartoon represent?

   d. What do the facial expressions suggest about the people's attitude toward King Monopoly?

   e. Summarize in a sentence the main idea of the cartoon on King Monopoly.

   f. What philosophy of big business is represented by King Monopoly? Explain your reasoning.

7. List several major social or economic problems that stem from laissez-faire and Social Darwinism.

Advanced Placement U.S. History 1
Lesson 28
Handout 28 (page 5)

Name_____
Date_____

8. Summarize the main idea of the cartoon on Andrew Carnegie's Gospel of Wealth.

9. Does Andrew Carnegie's Gospel of Wealth adequately solve problems created by those who employ the philosophy of Social Darwinism? Explain your answer.

10. To what extent do you see evidence of individuals employing either or both of the philosophies of Social Darwinism and Gospel of Wealth in today's society? Cite specific examples to illustrate your view.

Part B.

To conclude this lesson, assume that you plan to write a journal article reassessing the reputation of Andrew Carnegie and John D. Rockefeller for good and/or ill in shaping American society both for their own time and generations to follow. Include the following as an initial presentation to potential publishers:

a. Title of your article

b. Epigraph (quotation that sets forth your theme)

c. Introduction/thesis

d. Outline of evidence you will cite

e. Conclusion on the importance of your topic for readers today

Advanced Placement U.S. History 1
Lesson 29
Handout 29

Name_____
Date_____

The Impact of Industrialization on Workers and Their Families

Part A.

Select one of the individuals listed below and, for homework, assume the role of that person and prepare a two-minute presentation you might give before a House of Representatives committee investigating conditions in factories and mines and living conditions of industrial workers in 1895. Workers should focus on specific living and working conditions; capitalists should stress the benefits of unregulated capitalism in bringing progress to the nation; reformers should offer their insights on urban living conditions and any solutions they may have for improving living and working conditions.

Workers

1. a nine-year-old girl working in a cigar factory
2. a Russian Jew working in New York's Garment District
3. a female textile worker
4. a steel worker in the Carnegie steel mill in Homestead, Pennsylvania
5. a Serbian immigrant working in the coal mines in Pennsylvania
6. a male worker in one of Rockefeller's Cleveland refineries

Capitalists

1. Andrew Carnegie
2. John D. Rockefeller

Social Critics

1. Samuel Gompers, founder of the American Federation of Labor
2. Edward Bellamy, author of *Looking Backward: 2000 to 1887*
3. Jane Addams, founder of Hull House in Chicago and author of *Twenty Years at Hull House*
4. Henry George, author of *Progress and Poverty*
5. Jacob Riis, author of *How the Other Half Lives*

Part B.

After you have heard the reports before the House of Representatives, draft a bill that you believe would have helped to alleviate one of the worst abuses of unregulated capitalism in 1895.

Name of bill:

Objective:

Content of bill:

Proposed method of enforcement:

How it would have improved living or working conditions:

© COPYRIGHT, The Center for Learning. Used with permission. Not for resale.

Advanced Placement U.S. History 1
Lesson 30
Handout 30 (page 1)

Name_____
Date_____

Labor Unions—The Failure to Gain Public Acceptance

Part A.

For homework, use your textbook as a reference in completing the chart and accompanying question. Then read the documents in part B in preparation for a class discussion on early labor unions in the United States.

Questions	Knights of Labor	American Federation of Labor (AFL)
Who was eligible to join?		
What were the goals of the union?		
What were the union's methods of achieving its goals?		
What was the public's perception of the union?		

How does your completed chart help to account for the greater success of the American Federation of Labor than the Knights of Labor?

Advanced Placement U.S. History 1
Lesson 30
Handout 30 (page 2)

Part B.

Read the documents below in preparation for a class discussion.

Document A

"I regard my people as I regard my machinery. So long as they do my work for what I choose to pay them, I keep them, getting out of them all I can. What they do or how they fare outside my walls I don't know, nor do I consider it my business to know. They must look out for themselves as I do for myself."

Massachusetts Bureau of the Statistics of Labor, *Thirteenth Annual Report* (1883)

Document B

To the American worker, who hankered to be rid of the capitalist "boss," a co-operative "self-bossing" had seemed almost as desirable as the self-employment of an independent individual—until he learned by experience how hateful co-operators may be to one another.

Selig Perlman and Philip Taft, *History of Labor in the United States, 1896–1932* (New York: Macmillan, 1935), 4

Document C

One of the most profitable opportunities open to authors was to write for the great juvenile public.

The most spectacular exploit was that of Horatio Alger, Jr., who between 1867 and 1899 wrote 135 books for boys. His favorite formula of the poor but honest lad who rises by pluck and industry from rags to riches had universal appeal. According to one estimate the total sale of Alger books was about 17 million, but this can be little better than a guess. Even harder to estimate would be Alger's influence in sharpening the acquisitive instincts of several generations of American boys.

Nelson Manfred Blake, *A History of American Life and Thought* (New York: McGraw-Hill, 1963), 445.

Document D

This cartoon depicted the national view toward organized labor.

Copyright Culver Pictures, New York, NY.

Charles M. Dollar, et al., *America: Changing Times*, 2nd ed. (New York: John Wiley and Sons, 1982), 560.

Document E

In 1877, a year of violence in which a general strike threatened to halt national production, federal troops engaged railroad strikers in Baltimore. Scores of people were killed and millions of dollars in property destroyed.

Copyright Culver Pictures, New York, NY.
Charles M. Dollar, et al., *America: Changing Times*, 561.

Document F

Social-Revolutionary clubs made their appearance in New York, Boston, Philadelphia, Milwaukee, and Chicago, composed of foreign-born workers who had belonged to the Socialist Labor Party or who had recently arrived from Germany. Eventually the new organizations were to federate and form the Revolutionary Socialist Party. This party's platform, adopted at a convention in 1881, urged the organization of trade unions on "communistic" principles and asserted that aid should be given only to those unions which were "progressive" in character. The platform also denounced the ballot as "an invention of the bourgeoisie to fool the workers" and recommended independent political action only in order to prove to workers "the iniquity of our political institutions and the futility of seeking to reconstruct society through the ballot." The chief weapons to be used in combating the capitalist system were "the armed organizations of workingmen who stand ready with the gun to resist encroachment upon their rights. . . ."

Very few workers in America were full-fledged anarchists. In the main those who were influenced by the anarchist philosophy, were class-conscious, militant trade unionists, who had lost faith in the efficacy of the ballot as a result of the increasing use of troops and local police to crush strikes, the wide-spread corruption in politics, and the inability even to seat labor candidates when they were elected to office.

Philip S. Foner, *History of the Labor Movement in the United States*
(New York: International Publishers, 1947), 496

Document G

"I want to tell you Socialists, that I have studied your philosophy, read your works upon economics, and not the meanest of them; studied your standard works, both in English and in German—have not only read but studied them. I have heard your orators and watched the work of your movement the world over. I have kept close watch upon your doctrines for thirty years; have been closely associated with many of you, and know what you think and what you propose. I know, too, what you have up your sleeve. And I want to say that I am entirely at variance with your philosophy. I declare to you, I am not only at variance with your doctrines, but with your philosophy. Economically, you are unsound; socially, you are wrong; and industrially you are an impossibility."

Samuel Gompers
Perlman and Taft, *History of Labor in the United States, 1896–1932*, 151

Document H

It is idle to talk of a peaceable strike. None such has ever occurred. All combinations to interfere with perfect freedom in the proper management and control of one's lawful business, to dictate the terms upon which such business shall be conducted by means of threats, are within the condemnation of the law.

Judge Jenkin, *Farmer's Loan and Trust vs. Northern Pacific*, 1894

Document I

"Old-stock Americans often thought that others were strange, inferior, and potentially disloyal. . . . Rapid social and economic changes in American society after the Civil War reinforced intolerance. In the 1890s American nativists began noting with alarm the shifting patterns of immigration that brought so many Jews and Catholics from southern and eastern Europe. Labor violence, such as that occurring during the railroad disturbances of 1877 and at the Haymarket in Chicago in 1886, crowded slums in the nation's fast-growing cities, and industrial strikes also created uneasiness about the stability of American society. Nativists were quick to blame foreign radicals and agitators for the unrest. . . .

"Many others, reformers and nonreformers alike, feared the economic impact of immigration. When depression drove wages down and threw people out of work, they blamed the immigrants for lowering the American standard of living. Many of the newcomers, themselves prisoners of peasant ignorance and superstition, came with traditional hatreds and suspicions of one another, and they did not lose these feelings quickly in the United States. All of these conditions contributed to the widespread intolerance and bigotry that flourished in the United States during the late nineteenth and well into the twentieth centuries."

Leonard Dinnerstein, Roger L. Nichols, and David M. Reimers, *Natives and Strangers*
(New York: Oxford University Press, 1979), 220–221

Advanced Placement U.S. History 1
Lesson 30
Handout 30 (page 5)

Name_____
Date_____

Part C.

Assume the role of a Pennsylvania state legislator from Homestead, Pennsylvania. You have been asked to present the keynote address at the Annual Convention of the American Federation of Labor in 1896. As a former member of an AFL affiliate union, you have a unique perspective in that you are sympathetic to the working conditions of labor, you live in a community wracked by the Homestead Strike, and your new role as legislator has brought you an awareness of attitudes of business and the general public toward organized labor. Union leaders eagerly await your presentation on "The AFL's Potential for Changing Public Perceptions of Organized Labor." Prepare a poster listing your five most concrete bits of advice to union leaders as they plan their agenda for the next decade. Be ready to offer your rationale for these ideas in your presentation to the class.

Advanced Placement U.S. History 1
Lesson 31
Handout 31 (page 1)

Name_____
Date_____

The Farmers' Dilemma—To Produce or Not to Produce

Part A.

Read the documents below as a resource in answering the questions at the end.

Document A
Average Market Prices of Three Crops, 1870–1897

Years	Wheat (per bushel)	Corn (per bushel)	Cotton (per pound)
1870–1873	106.7	43.1	15.1
1874–1877	94.4	40.9	11.1
1878–1881	100.6	43.1	9.5
1882–1885	80.2	39.8	9.1
1886–1889	74.8	35.9	8.3
1890–1893	70.9	41.7	7.8
1894–1897	63.3	29.7	5.8

From *The Populist Revolt* by John D. Hicks, orig. 1931, renewed 1959. Reprinted with permission of University of Minnesota Press, Minneapolis, MN.

Document B

We were told two years ago to go to work and raise a big crop, that was all we needed. We went to work and plowed and planted; the rains fell, the sun shone, nature smiled, and we raised the big crop that they told us to; and what came of it? Eight cent corn, ten cent oats, two cent beef and no price at all for butter and eggs—that's what came of it. Then the politicians said that we suffered from over-production.

John D. Hicks, *The Populist Revolt*

Document C

It is not unfair to say that normally the railroads—sometimes a single road—dominated the political situation in every western state. In Kansas the Sante Fe was all-powerful; in Nebraska the Burlington and the Union Pacific shared the control of the state; everywhere the political power of one or more of the roads was a recognized fact. Railway influence was exerted in practically every important nominating convention to insure that no one hostile to the railways should be named for office. Railway lobbyists were on hand whenever a legislature met to see that measures unfavorable to the roads were quietly eliminated. Railway taxation, a particularly tender question, was always watched with the greatest solicitude and, from the standpoint of the prevention of high taxes, usually with the greatest of success. How much bribery and corruption and intrigue the railroads used to secure the ends they desired will never be known. For a long time, however, by fair means or foul, their wishes in most localities were closely akin to law. Beyond a doubt whole legislatures were sometimes bought and sold.

John D. Hicks, *The Populist Revolt*

© COPYRIGHT, The Center for Learning. Used with permission. Not for resale.

Document D

If the farmer had little part in fixing the price at which his produce sold, he had no part at all in fixing the price of the commodities for which his earnings were spent. Neither did competition among manufacturers and dealers do much in the way of price-fixing, for the age of "big business," of trusts, combines, pools, and monopolies, had come. These trusts, as the farmers saw it, joined with the railroads, and if necessary with the politicians, "to hold the people's hands and pick their pockets." They "bought raw material at their own price, sold the finished product at any figure they wished to ask, and rewarded labor as they saw fit." Through their machinations "the farmer and the workingman generally" were "overtaxed right and left."

John D. Hicks, The Populist Revolt

Document E

The Appreciating Dollar, 1865–1895

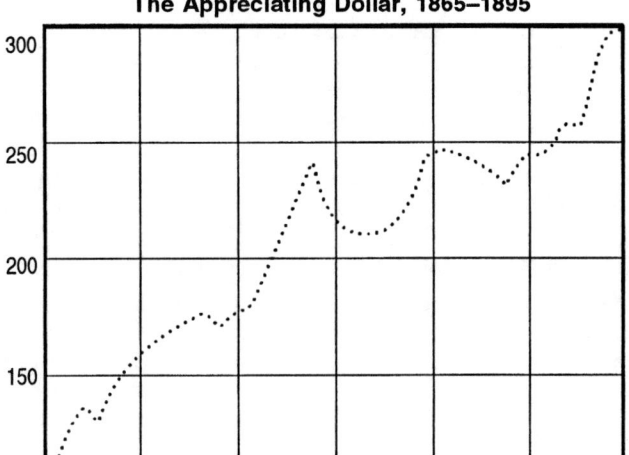

John D. Hicks, The Populist Revolt

Document F

Western farmers blamed many of their troubles upon the railroads, by means of which all western crops must be sent to market. There was no choice but to use these roads, and as the frontier advanced farther and farther into the West, the length of the haul to market increased correspondingly. Sometimes western wheat or corn was carried a thousand, perhaps even two thousand, miles before it could reach a suitable place for export or consumption. For these long hauls the railroads naturally exacted high rates, admittedly charging "all the traffic would bear." The farmers of Kansas and Nebraska and Iowa complained that it cost a bushel of corn to send another bushel of corn to market, and it was commonly believed that the net profit of the carrier was greater than the net profit of the grower. The farmers of Minnesota and Dakota were accustomed to pay half the value of their wheat to get it as far towards its final destination as Chicago. Small wonder that the farmer held the railroads at least partly responsible for his distress! He believed that if he could only get his fair share of the price for which his produce eventually sold he would be prosperous enough.

John D. Hicks, The Populist Revolt

Advanced Placement U.S. History 1
Lesson 31
Handout 31 (page 3)

Document G

As one hard season succeeded another the empty-handed farmer found his back debts and unpaid interest becoming an intolerable burden. In the West after the crisis of 1887 interest rates, already high, rose still higher. Farmers who needed money to renew their loans, to meet partial payments on their land, or to tide them over to another season were told, truly enough, that money was very scarce. The flow of eastern capital to the West had virtually ceased. The various mortgage companies that had been doing such a thriving business a few months before had now either gone bankrupt or had made drastic retrenchments. Rates of seven or eight percent on real estate were now regarded as extremely low; and on chattels ten or twelve percent was considered very liberal, from eighteen to twenty-four percent was not uncommon, and forty percent or above was not unknown. Naturally the number of real estate mortgages placed dropped off precipitately.

John D. Hicks, *The Populist Revolt*

Document H

The railroads controlled the elevators and warehouses, fixed the prices of storage, and arbitrarily graded the farmer's grain to suit themselves. Even when a railroad was honestly administered, the situation was no great help to the farmer, for usually the road had to make up for past financial abuses or for rate wars in other parts of the system, and this reimbursement had to come from freight revenues. Though freight rates were declining during the generation after the Civil War, they still were a third higher in the South and a half higher in the West than they were in the East.

Since the farmer had to absorb the middleman's percentage and the freight rates to the collecting point (Chicago for most important products), there were times when so little was left that it scarcely paid to ship. At a time when corn was selling at a dollar in New York, the farmers in Kansas were finding it cheaper to burn their corn for fuel than to sell it and buy coal.

Leland D. Baldwin, *The Stream of American History, Vol. II*
(New York: American Book Company, 1952), 199.

Document I

The Standard Oil Company of Ohio . . . had the advantages of different carrying lines, as well as of water transportation in the summer. Taking advantage of those facilities, it made the best bargains possible for its freights. Other companies sought to do the same. The Standard gave advantages to the railroads for the purpose of reducing the cost of transportation of freights. It offered freights in large quantity. . . . It furnished loading facilities. . . . It provided regular traffic, so that a railroad could conduct its transportation to the best advantage. . . . It exempted railroads from liability for fire and carried its own insurance. It provided at its own expense terminal facilities which permitted economies in handling. For these services it obtained contracts for special allowances on freights. But notwithstanding these special allowances, this traffic from the Standard Oil Company was far more profitable to the railroad companies than the smaller and irregular traffic, which might have paid a higher rate.

John D. Rockefeller, *Random Reminiscences of Men and Events*, pp. 108–109 in *Viewpoints: USA*, edited by Bernard Feder (New York: American Book Company, 1967), 202.

© COPYRIGHT, The Center for Learning. Used with permission. Not for resale.

Advanced Placement U.S. History 1　　　　　　　　　Name_____
Lesson 31　　　　　　　　　　　　　　　　　　　　　Date_____
Handout 31 (page 4)

1. From a farmer's point of view, what role did each of the following play in creating his economic hardships?

    a. Railroads

    b. Middlemen

    c. Bankers

    d. Trusts

    e. Government officials

2. How would each of the following groups respond to the indictment of farmers?

    a. Railroads

    b. Middlemen

    c. Bankers

    d. Trusts

    e. Government officials

Advanced Placement U.S. History 1
Lesson 31
Handout 31 (page 5)

Name_____
Date_____

3. To what extent do the documents suggest that farmers were responsible for their own problems?

4. What connection existed between the high cost of machinery and specialization in agriculture?

5. What happened to the value of money in the years between 1865 and 1895?

6. How would the appreciation of money adversely affect farmers with 20- or 30-year mortgages?

7. From a farmer's point of view, what might be a remedy for the problem of deflation?

8. Why would there have been strong forces in opposition to any government attempt to depreciate the currency in the late nineteenth century?

9. During Lincoln's administration, Congress passed the Morrill Act to create at least one land grant college in each state to teach agriculture and the mechanical arts. What help might a college such as the University of Illinois give to farmers in that state in the 1880s?

Part B.

Assume the role of Jeremiah M. Rusk, secretary of agriculture in the newly-created Department of Agriculture, during the administration of Benjamin Harrison in 1889. You have been asked to make the keynote address at the state convention of the Illinois Grange, the state's major farm organization. Your speech, entitled "Wake Up! It's a New World Out There," is meant to be informative, analytical, and helpful. Write the speech you would deliver to this group. Begin with a review of changes in farming in the last fifty years, explain why old solutions to farm problems will not work in the present, and suggest ways farmers and your Department can work together to solve the current "farm crisis." Create at least one visual to support your argument. Be prepared to present your speech to your classmates for their critique.

Advanced Placement U.S. History 1
Lesson 32
Handout 32 (page 1)

Name_____
Date_____

The Populist Movement—The Value of Third Parties

Part A.

For homework, research answers to each of the following questions.

1. In which presidential campaign did the Populists first appear?

2. What groups made up the Populist movement?

3. In what sections of the country did the Populists gain their greatest support?

4. List ten political and economic reforms the Populists proposed in their platform.

5. To what extent did Populists continue to focus on grievances of earlier movements?

6. What percent of the total popular vote in 1892 did each party gain?
   a. Republicans
   b. Democrats
   c. Populists

7. How do these percentages explain why the Democrats adopted several Populist planks and nominated the Populist candidate as their own nominee in 1896?

8. How did William Jennings Bryan's "Cross of Gold" speech prove to be both a strength and a weakness of the Populists?

9. How did Republicans try to project a universal appeal in their 1896 platform?

© COPYRIGHT, The Center for Learning. Used with permission. Not for resale.

Advanced Placement U.S. History 1
Lesson 32
Handout 32 (page 2)

Name_____
Date_____

10. What role might each of the following have played in the outcome of the election of 1896?

   a. Panic of 1893

   b. Republican party's $16 million campaign fund compared to $1 million available to Democrats for educating and persuading voters

   c. Some factory owners paid off their workers on Election Day and told them not to return to work on Wednesday if Bryan won; others threatened to pay their workers in fifty-cent pieces instead of dollars if Bryan won.

Part B.

Write answers to the questions below as your class discusses the following points.

1. Study the cartoon and answer the following questions.

   a. Why did these groups come together in a single party?

   b. How does the cartoon explain weaknesses of the Populist coalition?

From *Judge*, June 6, 1891 in *The Adventure of the American People*, 2nd ed. by Henry Graff and John Krout. (Chicago, IL: Riverside Publishing Co., 1970), 448.

© COPYRIGHT, The Center for Learning. Used with permission. Not for resale.

Advanced Placement U.S. History 1
Lesson 32
Handout 32 (page 3)

Name_____
Date_____

2. Why would a party with numerous issues agree to focus on the single issue of inflation?

3. Why did the anticipated victory of Bryan never materialize?

4. Why did conditions of the farmers improve in the years after 1896 despite William Jennings Bryan's loss in the election?

5. What Populist proposals later found their way into the mainstream of American political thought?

6. How do the following interpretations of the Populists characterize the movement differently?

> There is indeed much that is good and usable in our Populist past. . . . Populism was the first modern political movement of practical importance in the United States to insist that the federal government has some responsibility for the common weal.
>
> . . . Populists . . . bypassed and humiliated by the advance of industrialism . . . were rebelling against the domination of the country by industrial and financial capitalists.
>
> . . . [Populists sought] to restore the conditions prevailing before the development of industrialism and the commercialism of agriculture.
>
> Richard Hofstadter, *The Age of Reform from Bryan to F.D.R.*
> (New York: Vintage, 1955), 61–62. Reprinted by permission of Alfred A. Knopf, Inc.
>
> . . . Populism was indeed a response to the times, but it was also something more. It was an attempt to transcend those times and, in the act of transcending the existing social context, to pose an alternative conception for the development of America.
>
> . . . Thus, Populists contended, government must be a responsive tool, one which can actively intervene in the economy to regulate matters affecting the public interest, and when necessary own outright monopolies of this character, and can just as actively aid the underprivileged and work for a more equitable distribution of wealth.
>
> Norman Pollack, *The Populist Mind* (New York: Bobbs-Merrill, 1967), xxx, xliv.

7. To what extent does each interpretation have merit?

8. What conclusions can you draw from this lesson on the role of third political parties in American politics?

© COPYRIGHT, The Center for Learning. Used with permission. Not for resale.

Advanced Placement U.S. History 1
Lesson 33
Handout 33 (page 1)

Name_____
Date_____

Divergent Paths to Equality for African Americans

Part A.

For homework, use a research book or your textbook to answer the following questions.

1. How would you describe the political, economic, and social status of African Americans in 1900?

2. What factors explain why African Americans did not achieve total equality by the end of Reconstruction?

3. In what respects had the living conditions of African Americans improved since 1865?

Part B.

Read the following documents, and answer the questions at the end.

Document A

To those of my race who depend on bettering their condition in a foreign land or who underestimate the importance of cultivating friendly relations with the southern white man, who is their next-door neighbor, I would say, "Cast down your bucket where you are." Cast it down in making friends, in every manly way, of the people of all races by whom you are surrounded. Cast it down in agriculture, in mechanics, in commerce, in domestic service, and in the professions.

Our greatest danger is that in the great leap from slavery to freedom we may overlook the fact that the masses of us are to live by the production of our hands, and fail to keep in mind that we shall prosper in proportion as we learn to dignify and glorify common labor and put brain and skill into the common occupations of life. It is at the bottom of life we must begin, and not at the top. Nor should we permit our grievances to overshadow our opportunities.

To those of the white race who look to immigrants for the prosperity of the South, were I permitted, I would repeat what I say to my own race, "Cast down your bucket where you are." . . . Cast down your bucket among those people who have, without strike and labor wars, tilled your fields, cleared your forests, built your railroads and cities, brought forth treasures from the bowels of the earth, and helped make possible this magnificent representation of progress of the South. Casting down your bucket among my people, helping and encouraging them as you are doing on these grounds, and to education of head, hand, and heart, you will find that they will buy your surplus land, make the waste places in your fields blossom, and run your factories. While doing this, you can be sure in the future, as in the past, that you and your families will be surrounded by the most patient, faithful, law-abiding, and unresentful people that the world has seen. In all things that are purely social we can be as separate as the fingers, yet one as the hand in all things essential to mutual progress.

© COPYRIGHT, The Center for Learning. Used with permission. Not for resale.

The wisest among my race understand that the agitation of questions of social equality is the extremest folly, and that progress in the enjoyment of all the privileges that will come to us must be the result of severe and constant struggle rather than of artificial forcing. No race that has anything to contribute to the markets of the world is long in any degree ostracized [excluded]. It is important and right that all privileges of the law be ours, but it is vastly more important that we be prepared for the exercise of these privileges. The opportunity to earn a dollar in a factory just now is worth infinintely more than the opportunity to spend a dollar in an opera house.

Booker T. Washington, Atlanta Exposition Speech, 1895 in *Up From Slavery, An Autobiography* (New York: Doubleday and Company, 1902), 219–224.

Document B

The men of the Niagara Movement, coming from the toil of the year's hard work, and pausing a moment from the earning of their daily bread, turn toward the nation and again ask in the name of ten million the privilege of a hearing. . . .

First. We would vote; with the right to vote goes everything: freedom, manhood, the honor of our wives, the chastity of our daughters, the right to work, and the chance to rise, and let no man listen to those who deny this.

We want full manhood suffrage, and we want it now, henceforth and forever.

Second. We want discrimination of public accomodation to cease. Separation in railway and street cars, based simply on race and color, is un-American, undemocratic, and silly. . . .

Third. We claim the right of freemen to walk, talk and be with them who wish to be with us. No man has the right to choose another man's friends, and to attempt to do so is an impudent interference with the most fundamental human privilege.

Fourth. We want the laws enforced against rich as well as poor. . . . We want the Constitution of the country enforced. We want Congress to take charge of the Congressional elections. We want the Fourteenth Amendment carried out to the letter and every State disenfranchised in Congress which attempts to disenfranchise its rightful voters. We want the Fifteenth Amendment enforced and no State allowed to base its franchise simply on color.

Fifth. We want our children educated . . . and when we call for education, we mean real education. We believe in work. We ourselves are workers, but work is not necessarily education. Education is the development of power and ideal. We want our children trained as intelligent human beings should be and we will fight for all time against proposal to educate black boys and girls simply as servants and underlungs, or simply for the use of other people. They have a right to know, to think, to aspire.

W.E.B. DuBois, *Autobiography* (New York: International Publishing, 1970), 249–251.

Advanced Placement U.S. History 1
Lesson 33
Handout 33 (page 3)

Name_____
Date_____

Document C

The Booker Washington philosophy and program were the first positive ones that the masses of Negroes in America ever had. Previous to 1865 these masses had an externally imposed life-program which, for them, may be called negative in nature; almost nowhere in their lives had there been much opportunity or room for initiative, advance, growth, or maturity. . . . Here was the central and great wrong of slavery to which the beatings and other wrongs were subsidiary and symbolic. For most southern Negroes . . . slavery made true adulthood impossible. Limited though it was, Washington's philosophy and program had enough elements of positive though and action in them for the Negro to attain a type of adulthood under them, and in this sense, Washington offered an advance to his race and not a retreat. Washington correctly saw that for most of the freedmen even his philosophy-program was revolutionary, and thus it is that . . . he conceived of himself as a revolutionary leader.

Earl Thorpe, *The Mind of the Negro: An Intellectual History of Afro-Americans*
(Baton Rouge, LA: Ortlieb Press, 1961), 330.

1. How did Booker T. Washington and W.E.B. DuBois differ in their methods of achieving equality for African Americans?

2. Why were the policies of Booker T. Washington more acceptable to southerners than those of W.E.B. DuBois?

3. Use your textbook to find what methods W.E.B. DuBois and the National Association for the Advancement of Colored People used to achieve equality.

4. What difficulties would DuBois have faced implementing his program in the South?

5. How does Earl Thorpe account for the popularity of Booker T. Washington among African Americans in his day?

6. To what extent were the methods of Booker T. Washington and W.E.B. DuBois appropriate for the time in which they lived?

© COPYRIGHT, The Center for Learning. Used with permission. Not for resale.

Advanced Placement U.S. History 1　　　　　　　Name_____
Lesson 34　　　　　　　　　　　　　　　　　　　　Date_____
Handout 34

Arts in the Gilded Age

To gain a sense of the arts in the Gilded Age, create a short project according to the directions that follow. Leave one blank sheet at the end of your project so that you can add a brief analysis after class discussion of your research. This project will help you to review major themes of the period both now and at the end of the course as you prepare for the Advanced Placement examination.

1. For each of the following literary works, record the title, author, and a brief statement of its theme and significance to the literature of the period.

    a. Walt Whitman, *Democratic Vistas*

    b. Stephen Crane, *Maggie: A Girl of the Streets*

    c. Edward Bellamy, *Looking Backward: 2000 to 1887*

    d. William Dean Howells, *The Rise of Silas Lapham*

    e. Mark Twain, *A Connecticut Yankee in King Arthur's Court*

2. For each of the following architects, locate and photocopy at least two representative examples of his buildings of the period and write a brief statement on his philosophy of architecture.

    a. Richard Morris Hunt

    b. Henry Hobson Richardson

    c. Louis Sullivan

3. For each of the following artists, locate and photocopy at least two examples of the artist's major works and write a statement on the artist's career.

    a. John Singer Sargent

    b. James McNeill Whistler

    c. Mary Cassatt

    d. Winslow Homer

    e. Albert Pinkham Ryder

4. Finally, find and photocopy at least three examples of interior designs featuring Victorian style home furnishings.

© COPYRIGHT, The Center for Learning. Used with permission. Not for resale.

Advanced Placement U.S. History 1
Lesson 34
Handout 35

Name_____
Date_____

Arts in the Gilded Age—An Interpretation

Read the following interpretive essay on the Gilded Age. As you read, consider to what extent Leland Baldwin's characterization of the era fits evidence you amassed in your project.

> Americans were engaged in three quests—for wealth, for respectability, and for culture. The search for respectability found one outlet in the exhibitionism which has been called the cult of conspicuous consumption. No aspect of the Gilded Age was so clearly gilded rather than golden, snobbish rather than sound. Devotees of this cult made their headquarters in the brownstone mansions of upper Fifth Avenue in New York, but summered at Newport and wintered in the rising playground of Florida or the baroque palaces of the Mediterranean. Perceptive individuals, even among the wealthy, warned of the social and political effects of this flaunting of waste, but it did not lie down until the progressive movement and World War I brought in a new social consciousness and high taxes. In a sense the cult of conspicuous consumption flourished because rich men's tastes were those of the class from which they had sprung; simple, garish, untrained, and finding pleasure in a kind of juvenile display of superiority.
>
> Another and more valuable aspect of the search for respectability is found in what we may call the cult of respectability. There was considerable danger that slickness and love of power would become more prominent as American traits than the sense of ordered responsibility—that is, devotion to duty—which we call character. The task of subduing this wildness and of making character a part of the American grain was an absorbing interest of the Gilded Age.
>
> Reliability and predictability became the watchwords of the cult of respectability. Appearance, manners, and behavior became all important. The seamy side of life was ignored or covered with a genteel veneer; indeed there was a tendency to identify the appearance of respectability with character. It was not so evident then as it is now that respectability without character may fail in its aim, and produce a rascal or a stuffed shirt. Still, it was in the spirit of the English motto—"Manners maketh man." The attempt to teach respect for the humdrum virtues was a healthy sign and a necessary step to the building both of culture and of socially conscious wealth. It was also necessary in preparing the nation for the responsibilities which were to descend upon it in the 20th Century.
>
> There was something almost pathetic in the American desire for culture, and it was perhaps natural that the United States should tamely accept European dictates in art, music, architecture, and women's fashions. Even public taste in literature frequently waited on the British verdict. Women were most active in the pursuit of culture. Men were accused of being more uncouth: perhaps they were, but on the other hand it may well be that they saw that European cultural dictates were out of step with the necessities of the coming age. There was a saying at the turn of the century that the United States imported art and exported artists. It was tragically true that most Americans were unable to recognize the creative pioneers in their midst, especially if they had not studied in Paris, Munich, or Rome.
>
> Leland D. Baldwin, "The Gilded Age," in *The American Story* edited by Earl Schenck Miers (Great Neck, N.Y.: Channel Press, 1956), 235-236.

© COPYRIGHT, The Center for Learning. Used with permission. Not for resale.

Part 5
Transition to Modernity—Imperialism and Progressivism

In both foreign and domestic affairs America made a transition to what we might consider modern ways of thinking and acting in the early twentieth century. The lessons in part 5 focus on major United States' concerns at the time: imperialism, isolationism, and progressivism. America's emergence as a dominant world power shaped national responses to foreign affairs. On the domestic scene urbanization, industrialization, and immigration intensified numerous social problems, making the need for reform vital.

At the conclusion of this unit, you should be able to answer the following basic questions:

- What caused the United States to become involved in the Spanish-American War?

- What arguments did both imperialists and anti-imperialists present in the debate over U.S. ventures into colonialism?

- How did a colonial empire change U.S. foreign policy?

- To what extent did the background of Progressive leaders contribute to their successes and failures in the movement?

- In what ways did Upton Sinclair's *The Jungle* help to create consensus on the need for change?

- To what extent did the Progressive movement succeed in making government more democratic, business more competitive, and society more moral and just?

Advanced Placement U.S. History 1
Lesson 35
Handout 36 (page 1)

Name_____
Date_____

International Perspectives

Part A.

Complete the following research assignment for homework.

1. Research general information about political events in the following places at the given times.

   Annam, 1874

   Tunisia, 1881

   Egypt, 1883

   Marshall Islands, 1884

   Burma, 1885

   Samoa, 1889

   Rhodesia, 1895

   Mariana Islands, 1899

2. List other related information that you came across in your research or by looking up "imperialism" in the index of your text.

3. Write one paragraph concisely expressing a hypothesis you would make based on the information.

Advanced Placement U.S. History 1
Lesson 35
Handout 36 (page 2)

Name_____
Date_____

Part B.

Read the following statements of U.S. foreign policy and answer the questions at the end.

a. "The Great rule of conduct for us, in regard to foreign nations is in extending our commercial relations to have with them as little political connection as possible . . . Europe has a set of primary interests, which to us have none, or a very remote relation . . . Why quit our own to stand upon foreign ground?—Why, by interweaving our destiny with that of any part of Europe, entangle our peace and prosperity in the toils of European ambition . . . Tis our true policy to steer clear of permanent alliances, with any portion of the foreign world . . . "[1]

President George Washington's Farewell Address (September 1796)

b. "The American continents, by the free and independent condition which they have assumed and maintain, are henceforth not to be considered as subjects for future colonization by any European powers . . . we should consider any attempt on their part to extend their system to any portion of this hemisphere as dangerous to our peace and safety."[2]

President James Monroe's Seventh Annual Message to Congress (December 1823)

c. "Cities and towns have sprung up upon the shores of the Pacific. . . . Nor have we yet fulfilled the destiny allotted to us. New territory is spread out for us to subdue and fertilize; new races are presented for us to civilize, educate and absorb; new triumphs in the cause of freedom. North America presents to the eye one great geographical system . . .; it is soon to become the commercial center of the world."[3]

Senator Daniel S. Dickinson of New York (January 1848)

1. List terms that might be used to describe the thinking in these passages.

2. By the last quarter of the nineteenth century, these ideas had become traditional elements of American thought regarding national foreign policy. Do they reflect coherence or ambivalence? Explain your answer.

---

[1] Keith Ian Polakoff, et al., *Generations of Americans: A History of the United States* (New York: St. Martin's Press, 1976), 484.

[2] James F. Wickens, *Highlights of American History: Glimpses of the Past* (Chicago: Rand McNally and Company, 1973), 102.

[3] Frederick Merk, *Manifest Destiny and Mission in American History* (New York: Vintage Books, 1963), 29.

© COPYRIGHT, The Center for Learning. Used with permission. Not for resale.

Advanced Placement U.S. History 1
Lesson 35
Handout 36 (page 3)

Name_____
Date_____

Part C.

Read the following rationales for positions on foreign policy and answer the questions at the end.

a. "... the work which the English race began when it colonized North America is destined to go on until every land on the earth's surface that is not already the seat of an old civilization shall become English in its language, in its religion, in its political habits and traditions, and to a predominant extent in the blood of its people. The day is at hand when four-fifths of the human race will trace its pedigree to English forefathers, as four-fifths of the white people of the United States trace their pedigree today ..."[4]

Historian John Fiske (1885)

b. "Having therefore no foreign establishments, either colonial or military, the ships of war in the United States, in war, will be like land birds, unable to fly far from their own shores. To provide resting places for them, where they can coal and repair, would be one of the first duties of a government proposing to itself the development of the power of the nation at sea."[5]

"Control of a maritime region is insured primarily by a navy; secondarily, by positions, suitably chosen and spaced one from the other, upon which as bases the navy rests, and from which it can exert its strength. At present the positions of the Caribbean are occupied by foreign powers, nor may we, however dispersed to acquisition, obtain them by means other than righteous; but a distinct advance will have been made when public opinion is convinced that we need them. ..."[6]

Navy Captain Alfred Thayer Mahan (1890)

c. "The founders of this government—recognizing the difficulty of maintaining as a unit a republic of extensive proportions—inaugurated the Federal system, a union of sovereign states, hoping thereby to extend self government over vast areas and to maintain therein the purity of republican principles—each state ... of necessity containing a population ... of men capable of governing themselves. Therefore the founders ... made it an unwritten law that no area should be brought within the bounds of the Republic which did not and could not, sustain a race equipped in all essentials for the maintenance of free civilization and capable of upholding within its boundaries a republican form of government. ... Therefore, if we adopt a policy of acquiring tropical countries, where republics cannot live, we overturn the theory upon which this Government is established."[7]

Senator Richard F. Pettigrew of South Dakota (1898)

d. "American factories are making more than the American people can use; American soil is producing more than they can consume. Fate has written our policy for us; the trade of the world must and shall be ours. ... We will establish trading posts throughout the world as distributing points for American products. We will cover the ocean with our merchant marine. Great colonies governing themselves, flying our flag and trading with us, will grow about our posts of trade. Our institutions will follow our flag on the wings of commerce."[8]

Albert J. Beveridge, candidate for United States Senate (1898)

[4] Julius W. Pratt, *Expansionists of 1898: The Acquisition of Hawaii and the Spanish Islands* (Chicago: Quadrangle Books, 1936), 4–5.
[5] Pratt, 14.
[6] Pratt, 15.
[7] Merk, 244.
[8] Merk, 232.

Advanced Placement U.S. History 1
Lesson 35
Handout 36 (page 4)

Name_____
Date_____

1. List terms that might be used to describe the thinking in the first three statements.

2. What advantages does Mahan believe the U.S. might gain with acquisition of colonies?

3. Pinpoint specific convictions in Pettigrew's speech.

4. Identify the basis of Beveridge's position. How does he glamorize his thinking?

5. As the United States debated its position regarding Hawaii, the Philippines, Puerto Rico, and other territories at the turn of the century, what main points would each side emphasize?

    Imperialists:

    Anti-imperialists:

Part D.

Prepare for a brief class debate on the following resolution: The United States should maintain control of the Philippines in 1900.

Advanced Placement U.S. History 1
Lesson 36
Handout 37 (page 1)

Name_____
Date_____

Researching the Causes

Part A.

Research the following causes of U.S. entry into war with Spain in 1898. Add additional causes listed in your text. For each, describe the event and its importance in provoking the United States into war.

Causes	Description of event	Significance as a cause of war
1. The effects of the Wilson-Gorman Tariff 1894		
2. Cuban revolts against Spanish rule		
3. Pressure from U.S. businesses and their spokespersons		
4. Sinking of the *Maine*		
5. Influence of yellow journalism		
6. DeLôme letter		
7. McKinley's failure to prevent war		
8. U.S. public opinion		
9. A chance to fulfill our Manifest Destiny		

Causes given but not listed above

10.

11.

12.

© COPYRIGHT, The Center for Learning. Used with permission. Not for resale.

Advanced Placement U.S. History 1
Lesson 36
Handout 37 (page 2)

Name_____
Date_____

Part B.

Use the following excerpt from President McKinley's War Message to Congress and the Teller Resolution of Congress as resources in answering the questions at the end.

> ... The forcible intervention of the United States as a neutral to stop the war, according to the large dictates of humanity and following many historical precedents where neighboring states have interfered to check the hopeless sacrifices of life by internecine conflicts beyond their borders, is justifiable on rational grounds. It involves, however, a hostile constraint upon both the parties to the contest, as well as to enforce a truce as to guide the eventual settlement.
>
> The grounds for such intervention may be briefly summarized as follows:
>
> First. In the cause of humanity and to put an end to the barbarities, bloodshed, starvation, and horrible miseries now existing there, and which the parties to the conflict are either unable or unwilling to stop or mitigate. It is no answer to say this is all in another country, belonging to another nation, and is therefore none of our business. It is specially our duty, for it is right at our door.
>
> Second. We owe it to our citizens in Cuba to afford them that protection and indemnity for life and property which no government there can or will afford, and to that end to terminate the conditions that deprive them of legal protection.
>
> Third. The right to intervene may be justified by the very serious injury to the commerce, trade, and business of our people and by the wanton destruction of property and devastation of the island.
>
> Fourth, and which is of the utmost importance. The present condition of affairs in Cuba is a constant menace to our peace and entails upon this Government an enormous expense. With such a conflict waged for years in an island so near us and with which our people have such trade and business relations; when the lives and liberty of our citizens are in constant danger and their property destroyed and themselves ruined; where our trading vessels are liable to seizure and are seized at our very door by war ships of a foreign nation; the expeditions of filibustering that we are powerless to prevent altogether, and the irritating questions and entanglements thus arising—all these and others that I need not mention, with the resulting strained relations, are a constant menace to our peace and compel us to keep on a semi war footing with a nation with which we are at peace. ....[1]
>
> President William McKinley's War Message to Congress, April 11, 1898.

[1] Richard B. Morris, ed. *Great Presidential Decisions* (Greenwich, Conn.: Fawcett Publications, Inc., 1961), 318–19.

© COPYRIGHT, The Center for Learning. Used with permission. Not for resale.

Advanced Placement U.S. History 1
Lesson 36
Handout 37 (page 3)

Name_____
Date_____

The Independence of Cuba
April 20, 1898 (U.S. Statutes at Large, Vol. XXX, p. 738)

April 11, McKinley sent his message to Congress recommending intervention in Cuba. The Joint Resolution of April 20 authorized the use of the army and the navy to effect Cuban independence; the formal declaration of war followed April 25. The most important of the resolutions of April 20 was the fourth, known as the Teller Amendment.

Joint resolution for the recognition of the independence of the people of Cuba, demanding that the Government of Spain relinquish its authority and government in the Island of Cuba, and to withdraw its land and naval forces from Cuba and Cuban waters, and directing the President of the United States to use the land and naval forces of the United States to carry these resolutions into effect.

Whereas the abhorrent conditions which have existed for more than three years in the Island of Cuba, so near our own borders, have shocked the moral sense of the people of the United States, have been a disgrace to Christian civilization, culminating, as they have, in the destruction of a United States battle ship, with two hundred and sixty-six of its officers and crew, while on a friendly visit in the harbor of Havana, and can not longer be endured, as has been set forth by then President of the United States in his message to Congress of April eleventh, eighteen hundred and ninety-eight, upon which the action of Congress was invited: Therefore,

Resolved, First. That the people of the Island of Cuba are, and of right ought to be, free and independent.

Second. That it is the duty of the United States to demand, and the Government of the United States does hereby demand, that the Government of Spain at once relinquish its authority and government in the Island of Cuba and withdraw its land and naval forces from Cuba and Cuban waters.

Third. That the President of the United States be, and he hereby is, directed and empowered to use the entire land and naval forces of the United States, and to call into the actual service of the United States the militia of the several States, to such extent as may be necessary to carry these resolutions into effect.

Fourth. That the United States hereby disclaims any disposition or intention to exercise sovereignty, jurisdiction, or control over said Island except for the pacification thereof, and asserts its determination, when that is accomplished, to leave the government and control of the Island to its people.[2]

1. How did President McKinley justify United States' intervention in the war between Spain and Cuba?

---

[2] Henry Steele Commager, ed., *Documents of American History* (Englewood Cliffs, N.J.: Prentice Hall, 1973), 5.

© COPYRIGHT, The Center for Learning. Used with permission. Not for resale.

Advanced Placement U.S. History 1
Lesson 36
Handout 37 (page 4)

Name_____
Date_____

2. Why did President McKinley downplay repeated concessions by the Spanish government in making his request for war?

3. Why did Congress add the Teller Resolution to its plans to enter the war against Spain?

4. How could the United States reconcile its subsequent takeover of Cuba with the Teller Resolution?

Advanced Placement U.S. History 1
Lesson 37
Handout 38 (page 1)

Name_____
Date_____

A Foreign Policy for a New Age

Political cartoons are editorials in pictures. Interpret these political cartoons by answering the questions below each cartoon.

Cartoon A

The News Reaches Bogotá

Cartoon by Rogers from *New York Herald* Copyright 1903,
courtesy New York Sun, Inc., New York, NY.

1. What is the significance of the title of the cartoon?

2. What is the purpose of the gunboats?

3. Why is Roosevelt shoveling dirt on Bogotá?

4. Briefly summarize the main idea of the cartoon.

5. How might a Colombian cartoonist view the same event?

© COPYRIGHT, The Center for Learning. Used with permission. Not for resale.

Cartoon B

The Big Stick in the Caribbean Sea

Cartoon by Rogers in *New York Herald* (New York: Sun, Inc., 1905).

1. What is the significance of the title of the cartoon?

2. What do the boats labeled debt collector, sheriff, and receiver have in common?

3. To what U.S. policy does this cartoon refer?

4. How did that policy differ from the earlier Monroe Doctrine?

5. Summarize the main idea of the cartoon.

6. How was the "Big Stick" policy extended by Dollar Diplomacy?

7. How might a Venezuelan cartoonist view Big Stick diplomacy differently?

Advanced Placement U.S. History 1
Lesson 37
Handout 38 (page 3)

Name_____
Date_____

Cartoon C

Cartoon by Rogers from *Harper's Weekly*. Copyright 1899.

1. To what policy does this cartoon refer?

2. What is the main idea of the cartoon?

3. How might the Chinese interpret the situation?

4. How might the Japanese view the situation?

© COPYRIGHT, The Center for Learning. Used with permission. Not for resale.

Advanced Placement U.S. History 1
Lesson 38
Handout 39

Name_____
Date_____

Leaders of the Progressive Movement

Research Assignment

Name of your personality _____.

a. What vocation did you follow?

   (Examples: education, law, journalism, politics, etc.)

b. What was your background?

   - The extent of your education
   - Your religious training
   - Your relationship with your parents

c. What, if any, was the defining moment in your decision to become an active reformer?

d. What was your greatest contribution to the Progressive Movement?

e. Bibliography

Sample: William Jennings Bryan (March 19, 1860–July 26, 1925)

a. **Vocation:** A hypnotic public speaker, three-time candidate for President, and Secretary of State under Woodrow Wilson

b. **Background:**

   - Education—1883 graduate of the Union School of Law in Chicago
   - Religion—After struggling with the implications of Darwinism, joined the Jacksonville, Illinois Presbyterian Church. From this point on, Bryan never questioned the literal truth of the Bible.
   - Family—Revered the closeness of his family and projected this as a worthwhile objective for all Americans. He was devoted to his parents and learned from his father that the Democratic Party had the most concern for the common people.

c. **Defining moment:** Came around 1896 when he saw his calling and became an advocate for rural America against the Captains of Industry after the shocks publicized by the Greenbackers, Knights of Labor, anarchists, and especially the Homestead Strike and the Haymarket Riot

d. **Contribution:** Champion of all reform movements from income tax to Philippine independence; kept the faith that democracy can survive in a country no longer rural

e. **Bibliography:**

Anderson, David D. *William Jennings Bryan.* Boston: G.K. Hall Co., 1981.

Bryan, William Jennings. *The Memories of William Jennings Bryan.* Port Washington, New York: Kenikat Press, 1971.

Crunden, Robert Morse. *Ministers of Reform.* New York: Basic Books, 1982.

Glad, Paul W. *The Trumpet Soundeth.* Lincoln, Nebraska: University of Nebraska Press, 1960.

Advanced Placement U.S. History 1
Lesson 39
Handout 40 (page 1)

Name_____
Date_____

The Jungle and the Progressives

Part A.

The Jungle deals with many problem areas of the Progressive Era. As you read the following excerpts, record specific information dealing with these topics. Also list relevant historical facts.

Problem Area	Treatment in *The Jungle*	Historical Data
Meat-packing industry		
Political machines		
Child labor		
Plight of the poor		
Working conditions		
Unemployment		

© COPYRIGHT, The Center for Learning. Used with permission. Not for resale.

Advanced Placement U.S. History 1
Lesson 39
Handout 40 (page 2)

Name_____
Date_____

Muckraking and *The Jungle*

> "There is filth on the floor, and it must be scraped up with the muck rake; and there are times and places where this service is the most needed of all the services that can be performed."[1]

With these words, President Theodore Roosevelt, speaking to the House of Representatives in 1906, described the role of journalists and novelists whose works focused on the need for reform in politics, business, and society. Among these works is Upton Sinclair's *The Jungle*, a novel famous for its graphic descriptions of unsanitary procedures in Chicago's meat industry, as well as for its sympathetic presentation of poverty experienced by immigrants.

Near the beginning of the novel, we read of the hope, the optimistic belief in the "American Dream," that characterized the immigrants, including *The Jungle*'s main character, Jurgis Rudkus. Like many other immigrants, Jurgis expected that scraping together money for passage would be the biggest obstacle to a new life in the "land of freedom." Once in America, he would, of course, get a good job, marry, establish a family, and live the life of ease he thought all Americans enjoyed. Disillusionment came quickly when rascally agents, both on the ship and in New York, were quick to exploit him and his fellow Lithuanians as they sought jobs and lodging in their new country.

Jurgis and his "family" travel to Chicago, where they try to earn a share in "the good life" through various jobs in the city's famous meat industry. Sinclair bombards the reader with passages critical of the meat-packers. He targets graft and corruption:

> ". . . one evening the old man came home in a great state of excitement, with the tale that he had been approached by a man in one of the corridors of the pickle rooms of Durham's, and asked what he would pay to get a job. He had not known what to make of this at first; but the man had gone on with the matter-of-fact frankness to say that he could get him a job, provided that he were willing to pay one-third of his wages for it. . . . It was simply some boss who proposed to add a little to his income. After Jurgis had been there awhile he would know that the plants were simply honeycombed with rottenness of that sort—the bosses grafted off the men, and they grafted off each other; and some day the superintendent would find out about the boss, and then he would graft off the boss" (58–59).

The Chicago political machine also used the new immigrants:

> ". . . when election day came, the packing houses posted a notice that men who desired to vote might remain away until nine that morning, and the same night watchman took Jurgis and the rest of his flock into the back room of a saloon, and showed each of them where and how to mark a ballot, and then gave each two dollars, and took them to the polling place, where there was a policeman on duty especially to see that they got through all right. Jurgis felt quite proud of this good luck till he got home and met Jonas, who had taken the leader aside and whispered to him, offering to vote three times for four dollars, which offer had been accepted" (92).

---

[1] Theodore Roosevelt, "The Man with the Muck Rake," *Selected American Speeches on Basic Issues* (1850–1950), ed. Carl G. Brandt and Edward M. Shafter, Jr. (Boston: Houghton Mifflin Company, 1960), 279.

© COPYRIGHT, The Center for Learning. Used with permission. Not for resale.

Advanced Placement U.S. History 1
Lesson 39
Handout 40 (page 3)

Name_____
Date_____

Buying a house brought more abuses for unwary immigrants.

> " . . . as to the house they had bought, it was not new at all, as they had supposed; it was about fifteen years old, and there was nothing new upon it but the paint, which was so bad that it needed to be put on new every year or two . . . Cheap as the houses were, they were sold with the idea that the people who bought them would not be able to pay for them. When they failed—if it were only by a single month—they would lose the house and all that they had paid on it, and then the company would sell it over again" (65).

Sinclair's grim account of conditions and practices in the meat-packing plants caused many readers to become vegetarians.

> Jonas had told them how the meat that was taken out of pickle would often be found sour, and how they would rub it up with soda to take away the smell, and sell it to be eaten on free-lunch counters; also of all the miracles of chemistry which they performed, giving to any sort of meat, fresh or salted, whole or chopped, any color and any flavor and any odor they chose. In the pickling of hams they had an ingenious apparatus, by which they saved time and increased the capacity of the plant—a machine consisting of a hollow needle attached to a pump; by plunging this needle into the meat and working with his foot, a man could fill a ham with pickle in a few seconds. And yet, in spite of this, there would be hams found spoiled, some of them with an odor so bad that a man could hardly bear to be in the room with them. To pump into these the packers had a second and much stronger pickle which destroyed the odor—a process known to the workers as "giving them thirty per cent." Also, after the hams had been smoked, there would be found some that had gone to the bad. Formerly these had been sold as "Number Three Grade," but later on some ingenious person had hit upon a new device, and now they would extract the bone, about which the bad part generally lay, and insert in the hole a white-hot iron. After this invention there was no longer Number One, Two, and Three Grade—there was only Number One Grade. The packers were always originating such schemes—they had what they called "boneless hams," which were all the odds and ends of pork stuffed into casings; and "California hams," which were the shoulders, with big knuckle joints, and nearly all the meat cut out; and fancy "skinned hams," which were made of the oldest hogs, whose skins were so heavy and coarse that no one would buy them—that is, until they had been cooked and chopped fine and labeled "head cheese!"
>
> It was only when the whole ham was spoiled that it came into the department of Elzbieta. Cut up by the two-thousand-revolutions-a-minute flyers, and mixed with half a ton of other meat, no odor that ever was in a ham could make any difference. There was never the least attention paid to what was cut up for sausage; there would come all the way back from Europe old sausage that had been rejected, and that was moldy and white—it would be dosed with borax and glycerine, and dumped into the hoppers, and made over again for home consumption. There would be meat that had tumbled out on the floor, in the dirt and sawdust, where the workers had tramped and spit uncounted billions of consumption germs. There would be meat stored in great piles in rooms; and the water from leaky roofs would drip over it, and thousands of rats would race about on it. It was too dark in these storage places to see well, but a man could run his hand over these piles of meat and sweep off handfuls of the dried dung of rats. These rats were nuisances, and the packers would put poisoned bread out for them; they would die, and then rats, bread, and meat would go into the hoppers together. This is no fairy story and no joke; the meat would be shoveled into carts, and the man who did the shoveling would not trouble to lift out

© COPYRIGHT, The Center for Learning. Used with permission. Not for resale.

a rat even when he saw one—there were things that went into the sausage in comparison with which a poisoned rat was a tidbit. There was no place for men to wash their hands before they ate their dinner, and so they made a practice of washing them in the water that was to be ladled into the sausage. There were the butt-ends of smoked meat, and the scraps of corned beef, and all the odds and ends of the waste of the plants, that would be dumped into old barrels in the cellar and left there. Under the system of rigid economy which the packers enforced, there were some jobs that it only paid to do once in a long time, and among these was the cleaning out of the waste barrels. Every spring they did it; and in the barrels would be dirt and rust and oil nails and stale water—and cartload after cartload of it would be taken up and dumped into the hoppers with fresh meat, and sent out to the public's breakfast. Some of it they would make into "smoked" sausage—but as the smoking took time, and was therefore expensive, they would call upon their chemistry department, and preserve it with borax and color it with gelatine to make it brown. All of their sausage came out of the same bowl, but when they came to wrap it they would stamp some of it "special," and for this they would charge two cents more a pound (133–35).

Work began at an early age for children of the poor:

" . . . and so was decided the place in the universe of little Stanislovas, and his destiny till the end of his days. Hour after hour, day after day, year after year, it was fated that he should stand upon a certain square of floor from seven in the morning till half-past five, making never a motion and thinking never a thought, save for the setting of lard cans. In summer the stench of the warm lard would be nauseating, and in winter the cans would all but freeze to his naked little fingers in the unheated cellar. Half the year it would be dark as night when he went in to work, and dark as night again when he came out, and so he would never know what the sun looked like on weekdays. And for this, at the end of the week, he would carry home three dollars to his family, being his pay at the rate of five cents per hour—just about the proper share of the total earnings of the million and three-quarters of children who are now engaged in earning their livings in the United States" (71–72).

Layoffs that accompanied downturns in business threatened even the survival of their victims:

"For another ten days he roamed the streets and alleys of the huge city, sick and hungry, begging for any work. He tried in stores and offices, in restaurants and hotels, along the docks and in the railroad yards, in warehouses and mills and factories where they made products that went to every corner of the world. There were often one or two chances—but there were always a hundred men for every chance, and his turn would not come. At night he crept into sheds and cellars and doorways—until there came a spell of belated winter weather, with a raging gale, and the thermometer five degrees below zero at sundown and falling all night. Then Jurgis fought like a wild beast to get into the big Harrison Street police station, and slept down in a corridor, crowded with two other men upon a single step" (202).

The Jungle appeared in serial form in 1905 and in book form in 1906. Congress passed the Pure Food and Drug Act in 1906, and federal laws regarding meat inspection followed. The novel, then, is an example of a literary work helping to change history. All excerpts are from the 1981 Bantam Books edition of *The Jungle*.

Advanced Placement U.S. History 1
Lesson 39
Handout 40 (page 5)

Name_____
Date_____

Part B.

Theodore Roosevelt was, in many respects, the first modern American president. Unlike his predecessors who viewed their primary functions as chief executive and commander-in-chief, Roosevelt believed he had a role as a popularizer of reform and builder of public consensus for change. As a Republican, he preferred not to break up trusts and jeopardize the political and financial support of big business. However, as part of his "Square Deal" agenda for business, labor, farmers, and consumers, he did take steps to break up "bad trusts" who did not heed warnings that their business practices were simply unacceptable. Long before publication of *The Jungle*, Roosevelt had proposed regulation of the meat industry. He anticipated opposition from his party as well as from the industry. Although he wanted no part of Upton Sinclair's proposal for a socialist solution, Roosevelt took full advantage of the public's revulsion by the novel's description of practices within the industry to build his public consensus for reform.

To conclude this lesson, it is your task as members of the Cabinet to offer suggestions about how best to capitalize on public support for reform of meat packing.

1. Explain what arguments he should use to appeal to each of the following groups:

   a. Business

   b. Labor

   c. Farmers

   d. Consumers

2. Brainstorm a list of possible strategies for building public support for reform. (Remember that this is before the time of radio or television.)

3. Finally, create a flow chart showing when, where, and how best to use available resources to gain public support for the proposed reform. As you plan, you may find it useful to recall steps by which a bill becomes a law.

© COPYRIGHT, The Center for Learning. Used with permission. Not for resale.

Advanced Placement U.S. History 1
Lesson 40
Handout 41 (page 1)

Name_____
Date_____

Progressivism—Liberal Reform or Conservative Reaction?

Part A.

For homework, complete the chart below to indicate major political, economic, and social accomplishments of Progressivism at the national, state, and local levels. Be prepared to discuss in class the significance of each law or reform you cite.

	Political	**Economic**	**Social**
National			
State			
Local			

© COPYRIGHT, The Center for Learning. Used with permission. Not for resale.

Advanced Placement U.S. History 1
Lesson 40
Handout 41 (page 2)

Name_____
Date_____

Part B.

The question below appeared on a recent Advanced Placement examination. As with most A.P. questions, there is ample evidence to take either the affirmative or the negative position. To conclude the lesson, try to outline a response that agrees with the statement and another with a dissenting position. In outlining your answers, state your thesis, determine appropriate material to put the question in historical context, list the evidence you would use, and develop an appropriate conclusion that suggests the importance of the topic.

"The Progressive movement of 1900 to 1917 was a triumph of conservatism rather than a victory for liberalism." Assess the validity of this statement.[1]

---

[1] Advanced Placement American History Examination, Section II, Part B (Princeton, NJ: Educational Testing Service, 1987).

Acknowledgments

For permission to reprint all works in this volume, grateful acknowledgment is made to the following holders of copyright, publisher, or representatives.

Lesson 1, Handout 1

For use of maps from *The American Heritage Pictorial Atlas* copyright © 1966. Used with permission from Forbes Inc., New York, NY.

Lesson 4, 40; Handouts 4, 41

Advanced Placement test questions selected from 1987 AP American History Examination, College Entrance Examinations Board (1987). Reprinted by permission of Educational Testing Service, the copyright owner of the test questions.

Permission to reprint AP test materials does not constitute review or endorsement by Educational Testing Service or the College Board of this publication as a whole or of any other testing information it may contain.

Lesson 5, Handout 5

Excerpts from *The First American Revolution— The American Colonies on the Eve of Independence*, copyright © 1956 by Clinton Rossiter and renewed 1984 by Mary Crane Rossiter, Caleb S. Rossiter, David G. Rossiter, and Winton G. Rossiter, reprinted by permission of Harcourt Brace & Company.

Lesson 11, Handout 11

Reprinted with permission of The Free Press, a division of Simon & Schuster from *Interpretations of American History*, Volume 1, to 1877, Sixth Edition by Gerald N. Grob and George A. Billias. Copyright © 1967, 1972, 1978, 1982, 1987, 1992 by The Free Press.

Lesson 16, Handout 16

Thomas A. Bailey and David M. Kennedy, *The American Pageant*, Seventh Edition. Copyright © 1983 by D.C. Heath and Company. Reprinted by permission of Houghton Mifflin Company.

Lesson 16, Handout 16

Chart from *These United States, Volume 1*, Irwin Unger. Copyright © 1978 Little Brown Co.

Lesson 17, Handout 17

Excerpts from *A Shopkeeper's Millenium: Society and Revivals in Rochester, New York, 1815-1837* by Paul E. Johnson. Copyright © 1979. Reprinted by permission of Hill & Wang, a division of Farrar, Straus, & Giroux, Inc., New York.

Lesson 26, 31; Handouts 26, 31

Excerpts from *The Stream of American History, Vol. II* by Leland D. Baldwin, 1952. Published by American Book Co., New York, New York.

Lesson 27, Handout 27

Cartoons of "The Vulture's Roost," "J.D. Rockefeller and American Beauty Rose," "King Monopoly," and "Too Many Cooks Spoil the Broth." Copyright Culver Pictures, New York, NY.

Lesson 31, Handout 31

For John D. Hicks, *The Populist Revolt: A History of the Farmers' Alliance and the People's Party* (University of Minnesota Press, 1931), 2 charts and excerpts.

Lesson 32, Handout 32

"A Party of Patches" cartoon by Gillam from *Judge*, June 6, 1891. Found in The Adventure of the American People, 2nd Ed. by Henry Graff and John Krout. Published by Riverside Publishing Co., Chicago, Illinois.

Lesson 33, Handout 33

Excerpt from *Autobiography* by W.E.B. Dubois. Copyright © 1970. Permission of International Publishers Co., Inc., New York.

The Publisher

All instructional materials identified by the TAP® (Teachers/Authors/Publishers) trademark are developed by a national network of teachers whose collective educational experience distinguishes the publishing objective of The Center for Learning, a nonprofit educational corporation founded in 1970.

Concentrating on values-related disciplines, the Center publishes humanities and religion curriculum units for use in public and private schools and other educational settings. Approximately 500 language arts, social studies, novel/drama, life issues, and faith publications are available.

While acutely aware of the challenges and uncertain solutions to growing educational problems, the Center is committed to quality curriculum development and to the expansion of learning opportunities for all students. Publications are regularly evaluated and updated to meet the changing and diverse needs of teachers and students. Teachers may offer suggestions for development of new publications or revisions of existing titles by contacting

The Center for Learning

Editorial/Prepress Office
24600 Detroit Road, Suite 201
Westlake, OH 44145
(440) 250-9341 • FAX (440) 250-9715
http://www.centerforlearning.org

For a free catalog containing order and price information and a descriptive listing of titles, contact

The Center for Learning

Customer Service Office
P.O. Box 910
Villa Maria, PA 16155
(724) 964-8083 • (800) 767-9090
FAX (888) 767-8080